"OLE BOY"

Jim Bell raises a question from the floor at a CCL convention in Toronto in 1954.

"OLE BOY"

Sue Calhoun

Foreword by

Harry Flemming

NIMBUS PUBLISHING LTD

Nimbus Publishing Limited
P.O. Box 9301, Station A
Halifax, Nova Scotia
B3K 5N5

Cover Design: Kathy Kaulback
Photograph Credits: Marine Workers' Federation excepting:
    Chapter 12, page 93, and Chapter 13, page 101—Leo
    McKay; Chapter 14, page 109—Les Holloway.

Research and preparation of the manuscript was paid for by the Marine Workers' Federation, its locals, and Federations of Labour in Nova Scotia, New Brunswick, and Newfoundland.

Canadian Cataloguing in Publication Data.

Calhoun, Sue.

Ole boy
Includes bibliographic references and index.
ISBN 1-55109-017-1

1. Bell, J.K. (James Koval) 2.Trade-unions -- Nova Scotia --
Officials and employees -- Biography.
I. Title.
HD6525.B45C35 1992   331.88'092   C92-098588-2

Printed and bound in Canada by Hignell Printing Limited

CONTENTS

Acknowledgements vii

Preface   ix

Foreword   xi

Chapter 1: The Early Years   1

Chapter 2: Organizing the Unemployed   9

Chapter 3: Industrial Unionism Comes to
the Saint John Dry Dock   18

Chapter 4: The LLP and the Coming of the Cold War   31

Chapter 5: The Marine Workers' Federation is Born   38

Chapter 6: Purged!   46

Chapter 7: A Merchant Marine and the CSU   55

Chapter 8: 1950s: Canadian Supreme Court
Decision on Communists   62

Chapter 9: 1961 Strike   70

Chapter 10: The Co-op Movement   79

Chapter 11: Fighting for Legislative Changes   85

Chapter 12: Union Organizing   90

Chapter 13: Shipbuilding, Then and Now   100

Chapter 14: Reflections   107

Selected Bibliography   115

ACKNOWLEDGEMENTS

It was a comment I heard often when I started doing journalism in Halifax in 1977: "Someone should do a book with J.K. Bell." It wasn't until I met Les Holloway at a New Year's Eve party at Raymond Larkin's in Halifax in 1989 that the project actually got underway. Les had recently taken over as secretary-treasurer of the Marine Workers' Federation—a job held by Jim Bell for more than 40 years—and I was just finishing my book on the Maritime Fishermen's Union. It was a chance meeting—the result of which is the book you are about to read.

It goes without saying, of course, that Jim has been very involved in this project, as have other people. In particular, Hugh MacLeod, Sinclair Allen and Joe McLeod spent time "holed up" at the Hotel Shediac, inspiring Jim to recount his memories. I would like to thank them as well as Jim's long-time friends Gerald Regan and Harry Flemming for their help, Dr. Charles Armour and the staff at the Dalhousie University Archives for assistance in locating old photographs, and Dorothy Blythe of Nimbus Publishing for having the interest to undertake this project.

This, then, is the long-overdue story of the life of J.K. Bell, told in his own words as only Jim could do.

Sue Calhoun
Shediac, New Brunswick
Spring 1992

PREFACE

The Marine Workers' Federation undertook this project because it wanted to have labour's history recorded and told. Our history, and the labour movement's history in general, is very much a part of the history of this great country. Our children and our children's children must be given the opportunity to read about it.

The labour movement is about much more than strikes and wage increases. It is about a struggle to achieve social justice for workers in this country and abroad, and it is about people like J.K. Bell who committed their lives to this struggle.

Ole Boy is dedicated to working people everywhere. It is hoped that, as you read the sometimes humorous memoirs of this great trade unionist, you will come to understand some of our history, and how the labour movement has helped to shape Canada as we know it today.

Les Holloway
Secretary-Treasurer
Marine Workers' Federation
Spring 1992

FOREWORD

When I first met James Koval Bell more than twenty years ago, he was already a legend in Nova Scotian and Canadian labour circles. Since then, J.K. and I have shared many a jar, and at least as many arguments. Although a member of a trade union, I'm considerably to the right of him and a thorough disbeliever in the tattered tenets of Karl Marx. J.K. and I rarely agree on matters of political economy, but we've remained fast friends.

As he says, his schooling ended somewhere around grade five, an education that today would qualify him as functionally illiterate. He is anything but. He could find loopholes or flaws in a collective agreement or statute as quickly as any lawyer. He could write a brief to government with speed and insight. He reads much, if rather narrowly by my lights.

Although he was often accused of being a communist, J.K. never joined the party. I suspect if he had, he wouldn't have lasted long. He was too much the rebel. I used to say to him that if the communists ever took over Canada, he'd be among the first to grace a lamp post. Laughingly, he'd agree. I always thought J.K.'s socialism owed more to the Sermon on the Mount than it did to the Communist Manifesto.

His ideology was a product of the times in which he was reared, when hunger was real and "job security" a term yet to be coined. He knew the hobo jungle and was a pioneer in the literal fight to organize industrial unions. It was a time, as Woody Guthrie sang, "of guys and ginks and company finks." And it was a time when governments and employers brought in U.S. gangster unions, like Hal Banks' SIU, to take over allegedly communist, Canadian-based unions. It was a fight that nearly cost J.K. his life.

Through it all, J.K. never lost his zeal for making life a bit better for the common working man. Now, at 83 and in retirement, he scorns labour leaders who "ape the boss," drive "Mercedes Benzs" and affect "a hideaway apartment."

During all his struggles, J.K. never lost his sense of humour or his simple ways. Unlike many other labour leaders, he bought his clothes at Frenchy's–after checking for the union label. A few years ago when he retired as secretary-treasurer of the Nova Scotia Federation of Labour, I introduced him at a testimonial dinner with the note that we were happy he had come all the way from his modest Florida condominium to be with us. I said, "But in deference to J.K.'s socialist sensibilities, we'll call it a co-op." He laughed louder than anyone.

Another time when he told me he had sold his few shares in a local trust company, I asked him, "How can you, a branded communist (by no less than the Supreme Court of Canada), be investing in a clearly capitalist enterprise?"

"Ole boy," says he, "I'm trying to undermine the system from within."

This is a story that deserves the telling–and the reading. Organized labour is much different today than it was during J.K.'s long heyday. As heavy industry unions like coal, steel and shipbuilding waned in numbers but gained in working conditions, public sector and other service industry unions waxed in both numbers and remuneration. And their members have joined the middle class. These gains owe much to the efforts of J.K. and the ideals that he kept for a lifetime. From his standpoint, such progress is not without irony.

That Sue Calhoun has captured so succinctly so much of the life and times of J.K. Bell is a tribute to her. The rest belongs to him.

Harry Flemming
Halifax, N.S.
Spring 1992

CHAPTER ONE
Early Years

I was born in Halifax on October 18, 1908, the third of seven children. I had an older brother and sister, and after me there were three more girls and another boy. We were all fairly close in age.

My father's name was Daniel Bell. I don't know much about his family, other than that they were Welsh. He wasn't a very talkative person. He was an iron worker, steel worker, bridge builder, carpenter, pretty well anything that was going on. He worked a little bit as a blacksmith, and he could shoe horses. He could heat up metal. In those days, you really had to have two or three trades. If you relied on one trade, you would probably work a couple of months a year. Back then, only a small handful of men had full employment. The rest worked on a casual basis.

My father would think nothing of taking off to any place where there was a job, in Canada or the eastern United States. He would hear through the grapevine about a job here or there, in Boston, New York or Montreal, and he'd be gone. I remember he worked on a tunnel in New York. I don't know if it was the Brooklyn Tunnel or what. After the west side fire in Saint John, he went up there and worked on the footings to build new wharves.

When I was growing up, he wasn't around much. He would be gone eight or nine months at a time. Sometimes we went to see him. My father used to drift around. He wasn't bad but he wasn't the most model type of father in terms of assuming his responsibilities. But those were the times. It wasn't only him. He'd be down in Philadelphia. We'd hear from him. Occasionally a money order would come through and there'd be money to pay the rent. But it was never on a regular basis. You could never be sure of it.

My mother's name was Natalie Anne Koval. Her family was Ukrainian. Her father was a shoemaker. I think the family came over when my mother was one or two years old. They would have landed in Halifax and she grew up here. Her brother Bill was born here. I don't know how my parents met.

When my father was away, my mother would carry on. She would go out and work, doing housework for the middle and upper classes in Halifax. We didn't live too lavishly. I would go out and get wood. In those days, there was quite a bit of competition with the other young fellows to get wood, kindling for the kitchen stove. Everything came in wooden boxes so you would go to produce houses, wholesale outfits where things came in. It was free and every kid had a homemade cart to pull it in. That's what we used to heat the stove.

We used to steal coal, too. The coaling pier was right next to the shipyards in Halifax. The railway went through the shipyards, alongside what is now Pier 9, and out through what was then Africville, and hooked onto the main rail line coming out of Halifax. When we were kids, we'd go down there to steal coal.

In those days, we ate a lot of porridge, a lot of barley soup and a lot of fish that you wouldn't eat too much of today—shad, gaspereau, herring. They used to be cheap and plentiful. There were several wharves in Halifax, where the navy is today, and you could go on the wharf and fish. Once the fish were running, the word would get around and then there would be anywhere from 25 to 50 young fellows lined up at the wharf. You would have a fishing line and usually a bamboo pole. You used to wind the string around the top of the pole and then unwind it, just drop it down in the harbour. You didn't have the spools that they have today.

We lived in Halifax until I was around 9 or 10. I remember the good and bad things about it. I remember that Adams Transfer Transport had sleds, and each year the local kids in the community off Barrington Street and the north end would get sleigh rides. We used to go down to the pier where the boats came in from Europe and people would toss foreign coins at us. They would wrap the coins in paper money and throw them at us kids.

We used to think it was a lot of money but, of course, it was all worthless.

At that time, most of the houses had flush toilets but they'd be down in the basement. They'd have those pull chains. The toilets were damp because the basements had dirt floors. It was the next best thing to an outhouse. When you had to go to the toilet, you just went downstairs. We had cold running water in our house, no hot. The stoves were made so that the opposite end of your firebox was a reservoir that was kept filled, so that every time you lit the stove, you were heating up water to use for washing.

We had one of those galvanized tubs for Saturday night baths. We'd put the tub in the kitchen. You didn't change the water too often. All seven kids went into the bathtub before the water was changed.

* * *

I don't remember too much about the Halifax Explosion. It happened on December 6, 1917. After the explosion, tents were supplied and people lived on the Halifax Commons for the rest of the winter and most of the following summer. We lived in a tent probably for about a year. My sister Mary's eyes were hurt in the explosion. She was under a table.

I started school at St. Pat's on Brunswick Street in Halifax. I only went for one year or so. I don't remember much about my school days, to tell you the truth. I don't know why I left after a year. The household was disorganized or upset. It wasn't my decision. After that year, I would stick around the house. I would have different chores to do. When we moved to Saint John, I didn't go to school for about six months. We settled down and then I started again at Winter Street School and went up to about grade five.

The first job I had was as a newsboy for the suburban trains. The trains used to go as far as Hampton. There was a company called Canada News that had the contract to sell nut bars, peanuts, newspapers, things like that, on the train. They also had the concession in the railway station for the restaurant. You would get your stock from the restaurant and then you would go on the train and sell it. You would get on the train going to

MacAdam and go as far as Westfield and then catch the next train coming back. I did that all one summer. There wasn't much need for it in the winter because the traffic fell off.

After that, I worked for Jim Murray. He had been on a dredge up north and saved up his money and came back and bought himself a truck. Then he got a contract with the government to pick up mail from the trains and take it to the post office. The train originated in Charlottetown. Once it got to Saint John, we would take the mail off and take it to the post office. He also had a contract for express, things like lobsters and fox furs. We'd take them off the train and down to the boat to be shipped to Boston.

He had a large truck. I would sit in the front with him or on the back of the load. I was a youngster at the time so I was just a helper. I would work full-time, from about eight in the morning until the Boston boat left which could be around seven in the evening. We worked six or seven days a week and I'd make a fixed amount per week, around $8 or $9. It was under $10 a week. For a quarter then, you could buy three pounds of hamburger so we considered that good pay. A lot of people were unemployed so we were happy to be working.

Aside from that, I worked at anything that I could make a dollar at. We used to salvage shipwrecks and help to tear them apart. I was young and pretty big for my age. I was able to get by on a lot of these jobs for a while because of it, although sometimes my age would catch up with me. In those days, kids were a lot wiser. Keep your mouth closed. Don't talk about how old you are.

I was still living at home then and helping out. My older brother didn't work too much. He became quite sickly and died. My older sister used to work at the market in Saint John, helping people or selling, things like that. She went to vocational school, became a typist and worked for a lumber company. I think she was getting about $8 a week at the time for being a secretary.

I was 14 the first time I went on strike. I was working at a quarry outside Saint John, New Brunswick. It was a place along the highway that people called Torryburn. The quarry was owned by a Judge Adams. I don't know if he was a real judge or not. We referred to him as Judge Adams. He used to sell limestone to farmers. I guess he was getting a subsidy from the provincial government. Most of the employees were immigrants. There was about 40 or 50 of them. But because he was getting money from the government, he was under pressure to hire locally too.

So there were four or five of us hired. There was Stan Hunt, Jim Quigg, a fellow named Dino and myself. There was also a Vienneau. He had an old Model A that he had turned from a car into a truck. It was like something you'd see in *The Grapes of Wrath*. A couple of us would sit in the cab and the others would be in the back of the truck. It was about half a dozen miles from the city. Judge Adams used to pay us 25 cents an hour.

This one day, the immigrant employees got all agitated. They wanted a nickel an hour more. They said they wouldn't work and they were quite militant. So we rigged up a weight on the whistle—there was a little steam engine there at the time—so the whistle kept blowing after one o'clock. No one went to work. The men all sat around.

Judge Adams' house was at the top of the hill and he sent word down to find out what was happening. We said, "There's a strike on. The men ain't working." So he sent down that he wanted to see a committee. The immigrants were smart enough but they didn't want to be on the committee. They thought that we spoke better English and we should talk to him. So they elected three of us to go up and see the judge. We were the negotiating committee.

We went up to the front door and rang the bell. He ignored us so we rang the bell again. He barked out, "Go around to the back door." After a while he came out. He took one look at me and he said, "Were you ever in jail?" And I said, "No."

"Well," he said, "you soon will be at the rate you're going."

"Well," I said, "a fellow might as well be in jail for the amount of money we make around here." So he asked us what we wanted. We said, "Five cents more, 30 cents an hour." He said, "I'm not making enough money to pay you more."

"Well," I said, "the men aren't going back to work unless they get 30 cents an hour."

So we went back down again and he sent for us to come back up, mad as hell. "Okay," he said, "you're going to get your 30 cents starting next week." So we went back down, but instead of us being the bearers of glad tidings, the other chaps started arguing and fighting among themselves. What we didn't know was that under the table, secretly, the immigrant workers had already been getting 30 cents an hour while the local town fellows, we were getting 25. What they wanted to know was, was the five cents being applied to their 30 cents or was the rate becoming 30 cents? Were the four or five fellows from the city being brought up to their rate?

They insisted that we go up again and straighten that out. We went up again and that's when the judge really blew his cork. We said, "We're not going to work unless we get the same wages as the others." Boy, was he mad! Finally he said, "Everybody gets 35 cents." That gave us 10 cents more an hour.

It wasn't long after that that the city fellows were laid off. That happened around the middle of August and by September 1st the place was shut down. He kept some of the immigrants on for maintenance jobs, that kind of thing. That was my first experience in a strike.

After that, there was nothing to do so I took off up to Fredericton and got hired at a wood camp at Taymouth, east of Fredericton. The camp was operated by brothers by the name of Black. They were good fellows. They used to do contracting work cutting pulp and selling it to one of the mills. I went up and started cutting pulp. We got $3 a cord for cutting and piling. You were lucky if you got a cord in a day.

You cut with a Swede saw. There was a guy in the camp who sharpened the saws. He did that after hours because he was one of the cutters too. You gave him 75 cents to file your saw. All the gear that you used, like saw blades, was charged up to you. Everything you needed was in the "wagon." That's what they called the stores. After a while, the fellow who was keeping the wagon took off and the Black brothers, because they couldn't read or write, asked me to take care of it. I checked the order that was delivered for supplies, like groceries, to make sure that they weren't being overcharged. I also helped the camp cook. I did odds and ends.

I also had to double-check the scaler who worked with the paper company. He would come around and take measurements of the wood. He would mark the wood as unacceptable, non-payable wood because it was "red heart," he'd call it. They'd take it anyway when the trucks came but they wouldn't pay you for it. If you had a cord, he would say that you only had three quarters of a cord. So not only would the man who cut it lose but also the contractor. It was more or less up to me to argue with him whether or not it was good wood.

There were about 30 guys in that camp. We lived in log cabins that were put up pretty quickly. There were no toilet facilities. You just went into the woods. No running water or anything. Normally, a camp like that closed down in the winter. We were "spudding" the pulp—that means taking the bark off with a spudding tool—so that when they came to haul it away, it was just the bare log without the bark. After November, the wood sort of tightens up and you can't do that any more, so that's why they generally shut down in December.

Cutting the wood into four-foot lengths, you could usually do around a cord a day, depending on the size of the wood. If you got wood that was more than 12 inches in diameter, it would be easy going. If you got a bunch of small wood, it would take so much time that you just couldn't do a cord in a day. You did your own piling unless there was another guy working nearby and you had an arrangement to help each other. If you had a good day, you might make $3, although many times you wouldn't get that in eight hours. It'd take you 10, maybe more. You'd put in a few hours after supper.

If the guy running the camp was a religious type, he would close down on Sunday. The Black brothers were quite religious. We didn't work on Sundays but just sort of rested up. Lots of times we would go into Fredericton. Someone would have an old truck or we'd walk or hitch-hike, just to get out for the day.

They usually had a full-time cook. We ate pork, seafood, stews. They used to cook up beans the day before. When it was getting into the fall, they'd dig a hole in the ground and put the whole pot into the hole and cover it up. It'd cook in the ground. We ate heavy meals. For breakfast, we'd have pork and beans. And the same thing again for dinner and supper. Usually, there'd be lots to eat.

The guys would be anywhere from 15 to 60 years old. There were guys who spent their lives in those camps. They were a good bunch of guys, fellows who had worked out in British Columbia with the Douglas fir. They just drifted around. Usually, you were so tired at the end of the day that you didn't do much talking. By the time you got through eating, and went back to work for an hour or so, you'd be so tired that you'd just go and lay in your bunk. You had a big oversized gunny sack for your mattress and a blanket. You just fell down and went to sleep. There wasn't any electricity in those camps but we had kerosene lanterns. So occasionally, the guys would sit around and tell stories or play cards, poker or crib.

I was at that kind of work, off and on, for several years. I also worked at another camp down towards Fredericton, near where the Mactaquac Dam is today. By then, it was getting into the Depression years so anyone working who had cash considered himself lucky.

CHAPTER TWO
Organizing the Unemployed

I was probably around 15 years old the first time I went to Ontario. I rode the rods to get there. There weren't any jobs and I ended up in Toronto. At the time, the unemployed were just starting to get organized and being unemployed myself and being from this part of the country, I think you're more apt to want to be associated with people in any kind of a joint effort. So I eventually became secretary-treasurer of the Ontario Single Unemployed Union.

George Harris—he later became secretary-treasurer of United Electrical Workers—he became secretary-treasurer of the Married Unemployed Union. We used to co-ordinate our activities to put heat on the "onion farmer," Mitchell Hepburn, the premier of Ontario.

By this time, most of the unemployed were in relief camps— R.B. Bennett's 20-cents-a-day camps. Our idea was to get into these camps and get the people organized, to use the camps as a basis for political agitation, the same as they were doing in the US.

So we'd go into these camps. You'd get this Boer War issue greatcoat, clothing, a package of tobacco, a couple of razor blades a week. The camps were run by ex-army types and they were all anti-union so you had to be very careful. As soon as they found out you were trying to organize a particular camp, they'd expel you. So you'd have to change your name and then go down to another camp and check in.

Our objective at the time was to put pressure on R.B. Bennett to do something with these camps. The same type of camp had been introduced in the United States under Roosevelt. They were called Civilian Conservation Camps (CCC's). They were an outcome of the NRA—the National Recovery Act—which was a US anti-recession measure, and they were doing more useful things with their camps than we were doing in Canada. They were building highways, new roads, reforestation, things that were an asset to the economy, and they were being paid 35 cents an hour. In Canada, we had hundreds of thousands of unemployed in these camps and they were polishing up old statues and guns, and dusting off old military equipment for 20 cents a day.

So we were hollering, "Useful work at decent wages." That was our slogan. We wanted 35 cents an hour to do useful things. We said, "We should be building a TransCanada Highway." That was before the TCH existed.

We'd go into the camps and stay for a month. We were not prepared to stay longer because we were the organizers. We were there to make contact with people who would take the application cards, sign people up and set up a local of the Relief Camp Workers' Union. I was the general secretary.

We had our offices on Duke Street in Toronto. It was a sort of hostel for guys moving around who could come in, get a few meals and a place to sleep. People called us the "Duke Street boys." There were similar houses in other parts of Canada for the unemployed. We knew a number of people in political and academic circles who didn't want to be identified but who would help us out. We called them "angels." When we were short of money, we would indicate to them that we needed help to pay the rent, buy food or fix something up. They knew who we were and what we were trying to do. We'd take part in demonstrations or be in the newspapers for raising hell against the government but that wouldn't shake their determination to help us. Some people would say, "These are just a bunch of radicals," but the "angels" were the people who were determined to see us through.

We were in touch with fellows working with the unemployed in BC and Winnipeg. We also had a lot of contact with people in the US. They had some pretty smart cookies over there. We knew what they were doing because they put out these mimeographs or bulletins on their programs. They were carrying out the same kind of work, even though their camps were much more updated than ours and they were doing useful work. They wanted an expansion of what they were doing. But of course, like everyone else, Roosevelt pleaded a limitation on funds. Even under the New Deal, he couldn't put everyone to work. It was just tokenism or just enough to say they were doing something. There were still hundreds of thousands of homeless people. "Vagrants" or "transients" were still riding the rods.

It's probably hard to visualize but Canada and the United States at this time were both on the verge of civil war. For example, fellows were beginning to plan marches on Washington and on Ottawa. The general talk and general feeling across both countries was that people were close to revolution. I think Roosevelt recognized that. I think the American business people recognized it and that's why Roosevelt became president after Herbert Hoover. Hoover was a businessman and he just couldn't see any of the social problems that were developing in the country. Roosevelt was looked upon as an oddball, who was practising a little bit of socialism.

There was a lot of stuff going on that wasn't necessarily reported to the public—train derailments, damage at warehouses, places being set on fire so people could get food or other things. Things like that were happening in Canada, too. Times were gruesome, prices were high and people didn't give a damn. Fifteen or 20 men would break into a place for food. The authorities really didn't know how to cope.

In those days, there used to be meeting places along the railway tracks called jungles and you would have a couple hundred men jumping a freight train. The police would come down but there just wasn't enough of them. The guys would start throwing rocks or if some were carrying pistols, they would start firing. This kind of stuff was seldom reported in the newspapers. The authorities would know about it but not the public.

People were desperate. If it was cold at night, various places would be opened up for the transients, even police stations. If they got filled and there was no more room, guys would go down to a lumber yard, set fire to the wood and sit around all night. The police would know about it but would hesitate to interfere. You'd go into different places and they'd say, "What this goddamn country needs is a revolution and I'm gonna get the goddamn gun at home and I'm ready." That was common talk. People probably today don't understand it but, you know, people were homeless. Men, women and children were sleeping in the woods. They were starving to death.

I think in those days people had a higher level of political understanding than is the case today. There weren't a lot of the diversions that we have today, like television, so that if people wanted something to do, they'd go to political meetings. There were various left wing groups which believed that there was no need for the Depression, that there were plenty of resources. We were one of the richest countries in the world and we should organize the country in such a way that we shouldn't have a depression or welfare or these relief camps. Because of a lack of other things to do, people would go to these meetings and hear these debates.

For example, on a Sunday afternoon in Toronto, we'd go to Hart House. There would be some great debates, the left wing, the right wing debating various philosophies—communism, capitalism—right there on the stage of Hart House. I remember one meeting, the "Red Dean" of Canterbury, Hewlett Johnson, had just come back from the Soviet Union. Somebody in the audience started taunting him, saying, "How many Christians did you find over there?"

"Well," he said, "they don't preach Christianity over there but they practise it. We preach it a lot but we don't have a tendency to practise it."

It wasn't unusual for people in the audience to engage in the debate. If you didn't like what the speaker was saying, there would be a good exchange between the stage and the audience.

In those days, it was surprising how many people really believed that capitalism had lost its effectiveness, that capitalism had run its course and could no longer solve the problems of the country, that it was time for a new system, a new order. Some people were leaning towards fascism. Even fascists had large crowds when they called their meetings.

A chap named Adrien Arcand, the leader of the Nazi Party in Canada, was allowed to use the military armories in Toronto for his meetings. The fascists had no trouble convincing government officials to let them use the public armories all across the country. All the military would show up. They would be there in their uniforms. Usually a good sprinkling of the local police force would be in the audience and they would be hollering that what Canada needed was a good strongman like Germany had. They were anti-Semitic. They said that the Jews had all the money and that was keeping the economy down. The left wing people, the more liberal-minded people in the community, used to protest this. They were against what was taking place in Germany.

In those days, things were pretty black and white. What you had were the fascists, on the one side, trying to show you the advantages of the fascist system. In Germany, the trains were running on time, everyone was working, building the autobahn, the big highways. Of course, wages were low and unions were banned so there were no reports of disputes with the government or employers, and as a result, people were saying, "It's a form of utopia." No labour disputes, no unrest, everyone working.

On the other hand, you'd have the people who were attracted to the Communist Party because they felt that the system in the Soviet Union was working. You knew that there was a bit of repression but you'd excuse that more or less because you knew that there was a lot of sabotage going on. The western powers were attempting to finance counter-revolution. In a revolutionary period, all countries tend to go to the extreme, wiping out their oppositions. There were a lot of people over in Russia who were dispossessed but people tended to say, "So a guy who lived like a lord and had serfs supporting him gets knocked off, so what?"

So there was the right and the left and you pretty well had to make a choice. You had to declare yourself. You were either left or right. And the left wing movement was pretty pronounced at the time. It had quite an influence.

I was going to all these meetings and I became influenced by all these different philosophies. Gradually, I picked up a philosophy that was socialistic. I too felt that capitalism wasn't a democratic society. I still hold that view today. I think that capitalism doesn't lend itself to democracy. If anything, it lends itself to autocracy and towards an authoritarian-type of government. I think that's one of the greatest hoaxes ever perpetrated on people, that capitalism leads to a democratic way of life. I don't think it does.

I think capitalism has served us well. It brought us out of serfdom. I recognize the importance of capitalism as being one step forward, an advancement from the old days of slavery and feudalism. It provided a degree of advancement for people as a result of the Industrial Revolution. But I could never accept it as a model way of life, not then in the 1930s, not today.

I think this was a period that formulated my views in life. Since that time, I have recognized that my views are not shared with the majority and that there are different shades of capitalism, the same way that there are different shades of communism and socialism.

* * *

During this period, we had a lot of contact with the labour movement. I was knowledgeable about the structure of the trade union movement. I knew that there were craft unions and industrial unions. In 1934, John L. Lewis and a number of others formed the Committee for Industrial Organization (CIO). For a while, it was a committee under the American Federation of Labour (AFL) but it was kicked out. So Lewis and the others regrouped and changed the name to the Congress of Industrial Organization. And they started organizing industrial unions. They came into Canada under the wing of the All-Canadian Congress of Labour (ACCL) which had been formed in 1927.

Lewis did not hesitate to put left-wingers on the payroll of the CIO. He knew that some of these people would split their wages with others who weren't hired. Instead of having one employee, he would end up with three. People would do that because they were so committed to the idea of industrial unionism. They really felt that this was the solution to the problems in the United States and Canada.

I remember one of the boards of trade asked him why he was flirting with the commies, why he would put them on staff. And he came back with his famous retort, "Who gets the bird, the hunter or the dog?" In other words, the left-wingers were the dogs. They would get people organized and then he would come in. He was the hunter. And sure enough, that's what happened.

As soon as the job was finished, he just cleaned the left-wingers out. He made use of their enthusiasm and dedication and then he got rid of them. As unions became established and were chartered, the left-wingers were pushed out and the accountants moved in. This was much later, of course.

At the time I was in Toronto, most of the unions were either independents or under the AFL. The idea of industrial unionism was just starting in Canada. The CIO had the Steelworkers' Organizing Committee (SWOC) which was trying to organize steel workers at General Steelwares in Toronto. A number of us used to help them out. In those days, there weren't too many cars so most people lived within walking distance of the plant. We'd hang around and follow a guy home. Then we'd ask people in the street what the guy's name was and we'd compile a list of names and addresses which we'd turn over to the organizer. There were a few of us doing this so it wouldn't take long before we'd have a couple hundred names. So that helped them organize. In those days, you didn't do too much organizing at the plant gates.

I knew some of the people involved in the Workers' Unity League. They were up on College Street. We used to go up and visit their offices. Their group was much smaller than the ACCL or the AFL. They probably had about a dozen locals, mostly garment workers in the Spadina garment district. So we'd help them out too. Around 1935, they disbanded. I remember meeting a number of the Workers' Unity League people in the Congress in the early 1940s and they were in international unions then.

We used to go to meetings of the Toronto Labor Council. In those days, the labour temple was on Church Street. They had quite a place there, a great big pool room with meeting rooms downstairs and upstairs. The way it was laid out, the chairman sat up front on a pedestal, kind of like a judge, and members sat on two sides along the walls, something like a jury. The middle was vacant. I always got a big kick out of that because it reminded me of a British court, the Old Bailey.

We would go to Labor Council meetings looking for support for the unemployed or sometimes for money and they would give us certain little tasks to do. For example, in those days some of the unions didn't do their own picketing. They would get us to do it for them. Sometimes they would give a donation to our organization in exchange for us picketing. Quite often, we used to go down and picket with the garment workers in the Spadina garment district. The carpenters' union representative was Fred Davis. He'd have two or three contractors on strike around the city and he'd need three or four pickets. So we'd go out there.

* * *

One of the people who impressed me at the time was Albert A. MacLeod from Sydney, Nova Scotia. He was a very clever man, very well-educated. His father had been an official at the steel plant in Sydney. I think he was secretary in the YMCA in Canada before he joined the Communist Party. He later became an MP for Rosedale–St. Andrews for the CP.

Then there was Tim Buck, the Communist Party leader. I met him at one of the first meetings I went to in Toronto. After that, we saw each other quite frequently, dozens of times. He and I knew each other on a first-name basis. I also knew Stewart Smith and Reverend A.E. Smith, Stewart's father. Stewart Smith was a controller at Toronto City Hall. There was also Dewar Ferguson. He later became an alderman in Toronto. He was a member of the Communist Party. John Buckley was secretary of the Toronto Labor Council.

During the time I was in Toronto, I went back and forth a few times to Saint John. I'd hear that there was a job there, a ship that came in that needed a number of plates, and I'd slip down. I'd put in the winter, then I'd be laid off. The next spring I'd go back to Ontario and get elected secretary-treasurer of the Single Unemployed Union again.

I think the Depression years were very formative for a lot of the unemployed. When they went into the armed services and later into industry, I think it encouraged them to join unions. The fact that they had belonged to these unemployed organizations—not just in Ontario but in Quebec, BC and other parts of Canada— played a role in developing the organizational needs and organizational skills of people. It raised their consciousness but it also taught them techniques like how to hold meetings, how to pass motions, take actions, form resolutions, that kind of thing.

In a sense, the war was necessary, from the capitalist point of view, to solve the unemployment problem in both Canada and the United States. From a socialist point of view, I think we could have reorganized society to do the same thing without war.

Mackenzie King had said that once he got elected he would abolish the camps and provide work. Sure enough, after he got elected, he started to phase out the camps around 1935-36. By the time war broke out, the camps were still there but they were military establishments, filled with military men. At that time, I came back to Saint John.

CHAPTER THREE
Industrial Unionism Comes to the Saint John Dry Dock

Before the war, there would have maybe been a couple hundred guys at the dry dock in Saint John. Then war broke out and there were thousands. I went to work as a labourer, scraping ships and painting. I also set up keel blocks and helped the shipwrights. I went from being a labourer into the steel gang. I became a "backer out." I backed out rivets. Then I became a bucker, the guy on the other side of the riveter. Those rivets were white and hot. There were quite a few accidents. Later, I became a steel chipper and chaulker.

The dry dock in Saint John had been built in 1927. What happened, there was these two fellows, F.M. Ross and C.N. Wilson. Ross was originally from Scotland. He eventually got married to [former Liberal leader] John Turner's mother. He went out west after the war and became the lieutenant-governor in BC. Wilson was from New Brunswick.

Under the Dry Dock Act of the early 1900s, there was a subsidy available to anyone who wanted to build a dry dock at strategic places in Canada. I think the subsidy was $35,000 a year for so many years. So these two fellows got a government contract to build a breakwater in Courtenay Bay in Saint John harbour and they also got the subsidy for the dry dock. They went to work and took the rock out in such a way that they were building the breakwater and the dry dock at the same time. Then they floated a bond issue with Montreal Trust so that they would have cash up front for other investments. They used the subsidy to make the bond installments every year. So, rather than using the subsidy for the upkeep of the dry dock, like they were

Top and bottom: *A Parks vessel is launched at the Saint John, N.B. dry dock during World War II.*

supposed to do, they were using it to buy subsidiary companies like the Saint John Ironworks and Saint John Towing Company.

As a result of this, facilities in the dry dock were very poor. There was very little money spent on maintenance. When you went down to the dock to work you had to walk down these very crumbly steps. In the winter time, when it was icy, a lot of them would just break away.

Working conditions were terrible and safety conditions were practically non-existent. There was no such thing as issuing safety hats, safety glasses or steel-toed safety boots. They were all unknown at the time. When the steel was being ground or chipped, very frequently a piece of steel would go in your eye. You'd have to go to the first-aid fellow and he would take it out with the blade of a knife. There were a fair number of accidents and the odd fatality. I remember one fellow lost his hand in the plateshop. Guys would be killed when scaffolding would break. A crane would be lowering a plate down and it would hit up against the scaffolding and knock them off into the dock. The dock was well over 50 feet deep.

Overtime was a big issue then. It was quite a problem because of the amount of work in the yard during wartime. Some departments worked seven days a week. The employer was more interested in making the men work overtime than in hiring more workers because he knew that after the war he'd have to get rid of them somehow. Also, under wartime labour allocations, he could only get so many people. At the time, we worked 45 hours a week. We'd work until 1 p.m. on Saturday unless overtime was scheduled, in which case, we'd work longer.

Labourers were making 27 cents an hour. For journeymen, it was around 67 cents an hour. The dirtiest jobs fell to the labourers and there was an awful lot of it. The mechanics would insist that before they would go into a tank, it had to be cleaned out. So the labourer had to go into the oil tanks and clean them out with rags. Oil just saturated your body. When you came out, you'd be soaked right through with fuel oil.

Some of the ships that were brought down there were ones that Roosevelt had given to Canada. Newfoundland agreed to give the Americans a base at Argentia and in exchange, Canada got these destroyers. There were about 50 of them and some were in really bad shape. They had to be fixed up. They had been tied up in New York or Boston and the oil had jelled. It was like a black Jello. You had to go in and practically shovel it out. You had to flush out all the pipes and all the fuel lines and get them working again. It was a pretty dirty job.

During wartime, there were about 100 women working in the yard. Marker girls, we'd call them. In those days, there were plates that went on the sides and bottom of the ship. To make them, you put a template on the steel and the women had a little paint brush and they would daub where the plate was supposed to be punched out. Something like a pattern for cutting out clothing. We had women in both the Saint John and Halifax yards who were also welders. A couple of them up in the Pictou yard were riveters.

Alice Dickey [Jim's longtime companion] became their shop steward. They had a woman supervisor, Mrs. McIntyre. The women would come to the union meetings and explain that they were having problems with her, that they were being assigned to unfair jobs or that she was giving certain of her favourites the better jobs.

Alice was shop steward for three years. Then they began phasing the women out towards the end of the war and bit by bit they were shut out entirely. They laid off all the women. I don't think the women were too sorry because it was rather hazardous work, even though the money was good, more than they could earn in the usual occupations.

I should point out that these women initiated the fight for equal pay for work of equal value long before it became a national issue. As markers, they demanded and won the same rate of pay as the men after a bit of a struggle. So they broke the early ground in Canada on the equal pay issue.

There was a lot of drinking on the job in those days. In some cases, the employer supplied the booze because he needed guys to work. He'd say, "We gotta do this job, Friday night, all day Saturday." And some fellows would say, "Yeah, I'll do it if I can get a quart." In those days, the liquor was rationed. And if you didn't get to the liquor store, it would be all sold out of booze. I've known of cases in Halifax where fellows were given a crock by the general manager if they'd stay all night and the next day.

They'd be on the job sometimes for 48 hours straight, in the severest of weather.

Unfortunately, drinking was very much a fact of life. On Saturdays, fellows would come in, they would have been out the night before, and they'd always have a pint in their pocket as a kind of fixer.

Quite frankly, some of it was almost a necessity. You'd go down in the bottom of the dry dock and it was way below zero degrees and all that steel down there. The work wasn't necessarily continuous. Sometimes you had to wait for another tradesman to do his job, the welder or someone like that, and a lot of times you'd drink a pint of liquor during your shift just to keep warm. You'd be so cold that you wouldn't even feel the effect of booze.

Once I got into the yard, we started almost immediately to talk about unions. There was a group of us, although the others would leave it to me to make contacts and get the literature from the CIO and the ACCL. I would write away for it and pass it around. You had to be both an organizer and an educator because a lot of the fellows were not convinced that unions were legal. They thought that they were some sort of illegal conspiracy. Even the fellows who joined were not too sure. You had to show them the material, the recognition, the court cases.

The employer would try to overwhelm them by saying that it was against the law. I would be with them and say that that wasn't the case, and I'd show them court cases in favour of the union. This was before the time that companies hired personnel managers or spent a lot of money on lawyers. The companies and even lawyers didn't know much about labour matters. So if you could read up on these kinds of things, it didn't take much to become more proficient and more informed than the employer.

I was used to doing this kind of thing because of my involvement as secretary of the Single Unemployed Union in Ontario. I always took the secretary's job because it gave me the opportunity to write away for material and to make the official contacts. See, under the British system, the president is just an honorary position. He chairs the meetings. It's the secretary who is the sparkplug of the organization. Under the American system, the president becomes the key man of the organization.

Jim Bell in the early 1940s.

It's two different philosophies. But I always operated under the British system, with the secretary being the key person.

At the time, there was a small local of the Canadian Steelworkers Union in the yard but it only took in journeymen. The local was affiliated with the ACCL [which in 1940 became the CCL–Canadian Congress of Labour] that had been started because of opposition to international unionism and that was supposed to be a body of industrial unions, but this local acted more like a craft union.

We pleaded with the steelworkers to open up their books and take in more members. We argued that under their charter with the CCL, they were supposed to be an industrial union. But they said no. They weren't too sure how long the war would last and they wanted to keep their books closed. They took in men only by invitation or after they were in the industry for a few years.

So we started our own union. We called it the Canadian Dry Dock and General Workers' Union. That was around 1940 and we took in everyone who worked in the dry dock and shipyard who didn't already belong to a craft union. The steelworkers opposed us and wanted Congress (CCL) to recognize that they had the only charter in the yard. There was some hesitation on the part of the CCL because they weren't supposed to have two charters in one plant but they finally gave us one. A CCL rep in Moncton by the name of Roy Gould came down and interviewed us and sent in a recommendation.

So we got the charter and first thing you know, we outnumbered the steelworkers. So we suggested a merger. The steelworkers weren't interested but what happened was, the yard was expanding rapidly and one by one their members were being moved into supervisory jobs. When they saw their numbers diminishing, they finally agreed.

We had pulled out of Congress for a time because we insisted that there should be only one charter in the yard. We withheld our per capita tax, trying to force them to do something. So they sent down a vice-president, a guy by the name of Alex McAuslane, and he froze our funds in the bank. The CCL declared we were under supervision. It was a regular wrangle. All we were trying to do was get the Congress itself to live up to its own constitution

In 1942, the Canadian Dry Dock and General Workers' Union at the Saint John dry dock merged with a local of the Canadian Steelworkers Union to produce the Industrial Union of Marine and Shipbuilding Workers of Canada. The new executive, shown above, included Angus MacLeod (front row, centre). J.K. Bell (front, left) was business agent.

---

of being a congress of industrial unions. Any union chartered by Congress was supposed to be an industrial union and was supposed to be open to everyone who worked in the industry.

We took the position that the shipbuilding industry, because the employers were so resistant to unions, required an industrial union to deal effectively with the employers. The craft unions figured that we were a younger crew trying to stir things up, trying to upset the apple cart. But really, it was their own constitution that they were violating.

The whole issue was resolved by us merging with the steelworkers. After that, we were in good standing again with Congress. During this period, our local president was Randall Walker, a crane operator who played a solid role in the local leadership.

In the meantime, the Halifax shipyards had taken out a charter with the CIO under the Industrial Union of Marine and Shipbuilding Workers of America. So when we merged, we called our union the Industrial Union of Marine and Shipbuilding Workers of Canada. They were chartered through the CIO in the US but we were chartered directly by the CCL. We were approached several times by the CIO fellow in Camden, New Jersey but he said basically that they didn't have the time to service us. There was so much work to do on the American west coast with all the shipyards out there, they told us our best bet was to become directly chartered. After that, the Halifax local changed over to the CCL. They became Local 1 and we became Local 3.

* * *

In those days, there weren't too many distractions so we used to have a union meeting every week. Now the union meets once a month or every two months. There were enough issues coming forward and a lot of grievances so the meetings were fairly well attended. You had an opportunity to make contact with workers and give them general information as to what was going on in the labour movement and with the government, different bills that were being passed, that kind of thing.

This was wartime and the government was at least wise enough to realize that they didn't want too much confrontation with labour. Roosevelt had passed the Wagner Act in the US in 1935 that forced employers to negotiate with their employees' representatives. In Canada, we had PC 1003 which was basically a wartime measure. The idea was that the government would assume responsibility for ascertaining whether or not the union had a majority. You just had to satisfy government requirements, showing that the cards had been filled out and signed, and the government would certify you. So the need for striking to get recognition was eliminated.

Certain wartime industries were designated as essential so you couldn't strike anyway. You had to apply to the Wartime Wage Control Board to get your wages increased in order to keep up with the cost of living.

We couldn't strike but we did have occasional work stoppages. In those days, the yard had a number of young workers, boys of 15 and 16. We called them rivet passers, rivet catchers, sticker boys. They were quite supportive of the union. They were quite militant and they'd create hell if conditions were bad. They'd wildcat and when the rivet catchers stopped, everything stopped. The work couldn't progress.

The union would take them aside and explain to them that things had to be done in a disciplined way but it didn't matter. Some of them were even under 14 years of age. They weren't supposed to be in the yard but some of them were from poor families that needed the money.

We didn't get official recognition until 1941 although we had unofficial recognition before then. We negotiated with the company for overtime and piecework, among other things. I remember the first contract we signed. A labourer's wage at the time was 27 cents an hour, a journeyman's was 67. We negotiated a contract and got five cents more an hour for each. So one of the guys jumped up in a meeting and said, "Bell, you sold us out again." I said, "Why?" He said, "What did you take the five cents for? You should have got five percent." I had to explain to him that five cents was better than five percent, given that our wages were under a dollar an hour.

There was resistance all the time from the employer. He didn't want a union, although at the same time, he didn't want trouble in the yard. We had a few walkouts and a few shutdowns, just minor things. The employer was always anxious to get rid of the union. He would try to disillusion the men. He would offer a good job to one of the guys in the union and occasionally the odd guy would take it. The other fellows would say, "What the hell good is the union? All the union is just a way for certain opportunists to get a good company job and to hell with the rest of us."

When I worked in Saint John, I used to have to travel back and forth on the streetcar. I remember one time, Wilson picked me up in his car and he said, "You know, we have cars that we trade in all the time. We don't get much for them and they're in good shape. You're going back and forth in the snow and rain. We should sell you one of them for a good price." I said, "No thanks." That would have been the kiss of death for me.

For his time, Wilson was at least flexible and fair. His

ironwork manager, George Howard, was very fair to the men. After my refusal to buy a company car, my relationship with Wilson improved.

We didn't only organize the yard. We also organized half a dozen shops that were connected with the industry. For example, in Saint John, we had the Saint John Ironworks, a foundry that had also swung into ship repair. Then there was the Saint John Machine Shop, another Wilson company on dry dock property. It was making shells for wartime.

There was also J. Fred Williamson, a marine shop. The river boats and tugs used to be repaired there years ago. At one time they had about 100 employees. Then it narrowed down to about 30 after the war. They considered themselves doing the same kind of work as us but basically on smaller vessels, so they wanted the same wages and conditions. They became interested in the union. Old J. Fred had been an independent guy but he was dead. His son-in-law was running it. They were down on the waterfront where that big Hilton complex is today.

The guys used to invite me down to the plant so the boss would see me. That would be a gentle reminder that he better put a wage increase into effect or they would join a union. This was before we signed them up. They did that for a few years and it reached the point where our members, some of the guys on the executive, would say, "Don't go near them. The hell with them. They're just free riders." They were just using me to remind the employer that he should give an increase. But I would do it anyway. I would go into the plant and bingo, they'd get a dime more an hour. They eventually had some kind of grievance—somebody got laid off or didn't get paid right or something—and they decided they'd better join the union. There were probably around 60 guys there at the time.

There was also E.S. Stephenson. It was owned by an old established Saint John family. During wartime, they had electricians that did de-gauzing of ships that were in the convoys. They put anti-magnetic devices around the entire vessels so they repelled magnetic mines. These bombs that were in the water had a magnetic attachment to them that would attach itself to the ship, and then explode. With the de-gauzing, these bombs would be repelled by the ships hull instead of being attracted.

Once we got Local 3 going, we brought all these other little unions into the local. So Local 3 became a sizeable union in Saint John. There was a fair amount of interest in organizing unions in those days. What was happening was that prices were going up and wages were not rising. There was this no man's land with regard to wages in the smaller companies, whether or not they were covered by the Wartime Wage Control Board or not.

Local 3 had two business agents in a row, fellows by the name of Bill Cave and Jake Rooney. Neither lasted very long. One fellow took sick with TB and went into the hospital, and the other took a job as safety officer and went back into the yard. I think the job was a little bit beyond him. Then the boys came after me and said, "Jim, you started it, you take the job as business agent." So after a couple of years, I became business agent for Local 3.

At the time, the New Brunswick Federation of Labour was affiliated to the Trades and Labor Congress, an AFL organization. The president was Jimmy Whitebone who was in the movie projectionists' union. There weren't many CCL locals around and there was no provincial CCL federation. We didn't even have a labour council in Saint John.

* * *

One of the key fellows during this period was my old friend, Angus MacLeod who took over the presidency of the local. Angus was from Sydney, Nova Scotia. He had been secretary of an Ornamental Iron and Steel local that had been organized in the steel plant in 1917. A few years later, it was smashed by the company and Angus was blacklisted. So he moved up to Saint John, New Brunswick. He eventually got a job at the Saint John Ironworks. He was a tool crib man. He worked in the tool crib, passing out tools to the men. Just as soon as there was an opportunity to organize and get a local going, he played his part.

Just to give you an example what kind of guy Angus was. During the Depression, there were a lot of unemployed people in Saint John. Angus was working for G.E. Barbour, and at night, he used to go down and give some advice to the unemployed. Some of these people had worked for Saint John City Council in the summer but they were paid only scrip money. You exchanged it for coal and groceries and so much of it was held back for the winter. They wanted to get paid in real wages, 35 cents an hour, for the time they'd put in during the summer.

So they came to Angus and Angus used to go to their meetings and give them advice on how to organize, how to make demands, things like that. So anyway, a reporter attended one of their meetings and it came out in the paper that the unemployed were restless and that they were going to march on City Hall and that they had a spokesman by the name of Angus MacLeod. So George Barbour, the owner of the place where Angus tended the peanut roaster at the time, came to him and said, "Look, if you leave your job and go to that meeting tomorrow, you'll have no job to come back to." So Angus went home that night and said to his wife Margaret, "Here's the predicament I'm in." And he said, "What should I do?" And she said, "If you don't go and lead them, you won't be coming home."

To accost the mayor and City Council and make a demand on them in those days, well, that was something unheard of. But Angus led them down to City Hall and eventually they got things straightened out. I think they made a compromise that only fuel for the winter was held back and the rest you got in cash to have clothing for your children and groceries.

That's the kind of guy Angus was. He was a socialist.

CHAPTER FOUR
The LPP and the Coming of the Cold War

As I said, Local 1 at the Halifax shipyards had taken out a charter with the CIO in Camden, New Jersey back in 1937. But it didn't get recognition and didn't even get a first contract until 1941. Once we got the Saint John local going, we used to have regular contact with the Halifax yard, especially once they changed over to the CCL. You'd get in touch, find out what they were doing in negotiations, the usual interchange that you have between unions.

The leadership in Halifax at the time was H.A. "Pat" Shea, Alex "Scotty" Munro, Jim O'Connell who became the president, and Charlie Murray who was business agent. They were the spark plugs. The Halifax yard had an advantage over us in that they were more truly industrial than we were. At the Saint John dry dock, we already had these little craft unions operating. We couldn't afford to get into a fight with them. So we had said, "We'll establish our base among the ironworkers, the workers that worked on the ships."

We'd be back and forth to Ottawa for meetings with government. I remember one time we were there, Jim O'Connell and myself. This would have been around 1942. We had nothing to do one night so we decided to break into the government camp over in Hull where they had interned labour leaders who were supposedly communists.

We had one of those camps in Fredericton, too, although it was more for political leaders. The mayor of Montreal, Camillien Houde, was interned in it. What the government did was use these camps to intern anyone who didn't agree with what was going on. They picked up people at random, just to say, "You keep quiet or we've got a place for you." That's all that was, just a kind of threat. Charlie Murray—he'd been an organizer with the Canadian Seamen's Union in Nova Scotia—he was the one picked in the Maritimes.

Anyway, we decided to find out where the camp was and take the boys over some cigarettes and a drink. We knew a number of the guys who were there. We had a big bottle of navy rum. We thought we could hide it outside somewhere and try to get word into them. So Jim and I went over to Hull and we went into a bar and had a few drinks. And we said to bartender, "Where's that place where they're holding all those reds?" Somebody said, "Well, take the trolley coach there by Eddy's plant and go down to the end of the trolley line and walk about a mile past the end of the route."

So we found the gate to the camp but there was no one there. We went through the guard office and ducked into one of sleeping quarters. A couple of guys were there shining their shoes and we said, "Where the hell is everybody?" They said, "They're over in kitchen-mess area." So we went over and here were a couple of older guys, veterans of World War I who were guards at the camp. They had their jackets off and they were playing cards with the boys and drinking homebrew. When they saw us, they jumped up and grabbed their guns. "Who are you, what are you doing here?" Putting on an official act.

By then, a couple of the boys recognized us and yelled out. The guards saw that they knew us and we immediately produced the rum and the cigarettes. So the guards said nothing and offered us some of their homebrew. So we stayed there talking to the boys and drinking. When we left, the trolley car had stopped running. There was no way to get back to the hotel. It was war-time and there were no taxis. We had to hike all the way back. By the time we got there, it was pretty early in the morning. We said, "To hell, we're not going to go to sleep," and we opened up another bottle of booze.

We had an appointment with Mackenzie King and Humphrey Mitchell—he was labour minister at the time—at nine in the morning. We wanted to talk to them about conditions in the shipyards. So during the course of our meeting, we got into a big argument. We said, "The guys in the shipyards are making 67 cents an hour. The cost of living in Halifax and Saint John is just out of this world. The cities are overloaded with the military and people are renting out their attics, their cellars, everything. Restaurant prices are sky-high. Everyone who's selling something or renting a room is thumbing his nose at price control. Prices have gone up 300 percent."

Incidentally, the night before, I had had bacon and eggs at the camp until it was coming out my ears. I hadn't seen bacon and eggs in six months. So Mitchell butted in and he said, "Just calm down, we've got a place across the river for guys like you."

It was just on the tip of my tongue to say, "Yeah, I know. I've been there. It was the first time I had bacon and eggs in six months." Jim O'Connell kicked me in the leg, under the table, to keep me quiet.

* * *

During this period, I joined the Labor-Progressive Party (LPP). The Communist Party had been outlawed during the war. Up until then, I really hadn't taken too much time to become personally involved to any great extent other than going to a lot of meetings, sometimes for no reason other than to get out of the weather. I was never a card-carrying communist although I recognized the role that it played in society as a necessary one. It articulated the alternative to capitalism.

At the time, the Co-operative Commonwealth Federation (CCF) was more religious-oriented. Most of the people in it were connected to the United or Baptist Church, even though David Lewis, who was secretary-treasurer at the time, was Jewish. The party was based more on praying and "I beseech you," you know, to uplift the conditions of the working class. I was a little bit too militant for that. I saw it as a reformist party, not a party for basic change.

I realized that the time would come, however, when I had to take a stand so I became part of the LPP. It was founded in Toronto in 1942. It was a coalition of left wing CCF'ers and socialists and communists, people who felt that there had to be some kind of organized party in the country. It was a mass party that would take in the trade unions and other groups across the country. Women's groups were just forming around that time. So once it got started in Toronto, we set up a Nova Scotia chapter. I became the secretary-treasurer.

We operated openly. We had speakers, largely trade unionists in Nova Scotia. It was a mobilization of people preparing for the post-war period, but in Nova Scotia it only lasted until around 1947, then it kind of just petered out. I think it continued for a few years afterwards in other places in Canada.

My involvement in the LPP tagged me as a left-winger. That, and my willingness to listen and learn. I would go to meetings and I never took the position that any one particular group had all the answers. I was always open to new ideas.

The other thing that tagged us as subversive was the fact that we were an industrial union and a Canadian union. The fellows from the international unions would get up at conventions and make speeches about the left-wingers wrapping themselves in the Canadian flag, making out that we were loyal to the country when really our hearts belonged to the 'hammer and sickle.' Quite frankly, if living under the 'hammer and sickle' was as dirty as they were making it appear, I'm sure that we would have fought the 'hammer and sickle' equally as hard.

Nobody could stand the national unions. The employer would sneer at us, "Why do you send your dues across the border to the US?" But when we wanted to form a Canadian union, they would be the first to connive with the international unions to make a deal, even though the national one had the majority of workers. It was the same with the federal government. It didn't trust national unions.

This was the beginning of the Cold War which was reaching its tentacles into all phases of life, even the trade union movement. By 1946, the Taft–Hartley Act had been passed, that if you were a communist you couldn't be an officer in a union. That kind of established the climate all over the western world. There was no similar law passed in Canada although many of the provincial labour relations boards were applying the same principle.

There was a degree of cannibalism in the labour movement. Some unions were on the bandwagon to take over unions that

CONGRESS OF LABOR GETS READY TO TOSS OUT REDS

WINNNIPEG, Sept. 22 - (CP) — A new Red purge was shaping up tonight in Canada's second-biggest labor body.

The 360,000-member Canadian Congress of Labor was getting set to throw out its Communist-dominated unions, now reduced to a scattering as the result of rough anti-Red measures of the last few years.

The move will be somewhat similar—though with variations—to that of the Trades and Labor Congress of Canada in deciding last week to clean house of Reds in its 500,000 membership.

The executive council of the C.C.L., it was learned today, will propose to its convention next week that it be given authority to suspend Communist-dominated affiliates.

This move would immediately place in jeopardy several organizations apart from the big United Electrical Workers of America, which already is under suspension from the C.C.L. and expected to be thrown out completely at the convention opening Monday.

Bodies that might be endangered would be the Red-led Fur and Leather Workers' Union, with 5,000 members; the British Columbia Shipyard Workers' Federation, with 3,000 members, and the Maritime Marine Workers' Federation, a smaller organization.

The C.C.L. proposal, it is understood, will give unions barred by its executive council the right of appeal to the convention as a whole.

The move will not apply at next week's convention, when the left wing unions will be permitted to attend the deliberations. But they may find themselves in difficulty at next year's session.

The exception next week will be the United Electrical Workers, which will not be allowed to have delegates on the floor of the civic auditorium unless it can convince the 700-odd delegates the executive was wrong in putting it under suspension.

That suspension was imposed for alleged delay in paying the left wing union's monthly per capita dues to the Congress—a device to kick out the union since there now is nothing in the C.C.L. constitution authorizing expulsion for Communism.

The resolution to be introduced next week is expected to remedy that, making Communist domination of a union a specific ground for its suspension by the executive council and eventual expulsion by the full convention.

(undated, probably late 1940s, early 1950s)

---

were considered to be led by subversives. You had to constantly look over your shoulder all the time to see that they weren't after your members.

* * *

One time we went up to Ottawa, we were with Pat Shea—he was a representative for the Canadian Congress of Labour (CCL) at the time—and we went in to see Humphrey Mitchell. This would have been in 1944. Later, in the hotel, Pat was up in his room having a couple and he said, "Watch this. We'll have a little fun." So he called up one of the other fellows who was with us, Willie Comeau from Digby County, and he put on a British accent like Humphrey Mitchell and he said, "Mr. Comeau, what are you doing in Ottawa with these communists?" We found out later that Willie dropped the phone. "He called me a communist," he said.

So later, we went into Willie's room and we told him not to worry. It was only Pat Shea. And we said, "We'll see if he can take it." So a few of us got together and scribbled out a telegram: "Membership in Halifax greatly disturbed over reports that you and other members of the delegation to Ottawa and Hull arrested for drunkenness. Please send wire immediately confirming or denying same. Signed, Charlie Murray." Charlie was the union's business agent in Halifax at the time.

So we went downstairs to a pay phone and called it in. They wrote it down and then put it in an envelope and took it up to Pat's room. So Pat got this telegram. "That son of a bitch," he says, "I knew Murray was out to get me. There he is, spreading lies." So anyway, he started dashing off a big long letter to Murray that he was going to put him up on charges before the CCL. He was sending a copy to Conroy and Mosher and the whole works. Finally we had to stop him and explain that it had been a practical joke.

* * *

I remember one time when George MacEachern, president of the local at the shipyards in Pictou, and Dan L. MacDonald, who was also in the union, gave me a call. Very urgent, I must come down to Pictou. In those days, I had no car so I took the train from Saint John up to Moncton and then got the train to Halifax and went down as far as Oxford Junction and then took the shore line down to Pictou. It was kind of a tedious journey but I thought to myself, "Well, I'll get there as fast as I can and see what the problem is."

Well, I got there and here Dan and George had been on a toot—their wives were away up in Cape Breton—and they were into a big argument as to whether or not Lenin was right when he introduced his five-year plan in the Soviet Union, when he made industrialization a priority. They were into a fight and they wanted me to referee. There were all these homebrew bottles scattered all over the floor. At that time I wasn't drinking too much and homebrew wasn't too appealing to me. But then we got into the real stuff and it took a couple of days to settle that argument.

* * *

What appealed to me and to a lot of people about the Communist Party was its militancy. The fact that it stood up to R.B. Bennett and his right wing positions. Although the other parties may not have agreed with Bennett and his duplicity, they weren't in the forefront of confrontation. The Communist Party was. Being a militant, I was naturally more attracted to it.

Why did I never join? It was probably because of the fact that in the Maritimes there was never really an active organization. It was mainly active in Ontario and Quebec and in western Canada. The other thing was there was an awful lot of bickering within the party about whether or not this fellow or the other was an agent of the RCMP. There were also a lot of internal disputes, and I thought, "I'm not going to be part of that."

People had the idea that the further left you go, the more serene it is because you're just subject to orders from above. But that wasn't the case. There was a constant turmoil of debate, internal division on policy and tactics. I didn't want to get caught up in all that. I wanted to concentrate on building a strong base for the labour movement in the Maritimes. I was hustling around, trying to get locals organized. At one point, we had four locals up for certification at the same time. Very few unions had that. This was in the early 1950s.

So I never joined the Communist Party although a lot of people assumed that I had.

CHAPTER FIVE
The Marine Workers' Federation is Born

During wartime, no one wanted a strike. The Halifax local had been asking Dosco [Dominion Coal and Steel Corporation Ltd.—owners of the Halifax shipyards] for check-off for about three years. It wanted the company to automatically deduct dues and submit them to the union, rather than the union having to collect dues individually from every member. But the company had refused. So finally, the local pulled a strike in August 1944.

The coal miners in Cape Breton had had check-off for years and they had won it through their own efforts in collective bargaining. In 1937, the Nova Scotia government passed the trade union act. It was the first trade union act of any provincial government in Canada and it included a provision for check-off.

This was the one gift that Angus L. Macdonald gave to the working people of Nova Scotia, the one big reform that he made. I think Angus L. could foresee a lot of fights ahead with Dosco in particular. Dosco had a lot of holdings—the steel plant in Trenton, the shipyards in Halifax, the steel plant in Sydney—and a lot of the Dosco units were on the verge of being organized by the Steelworkers' Organizing Committee. Angus L. was astute enough to know that if the steelworkers had a strike for check-off, they would get the support of the miners. At the time, steel and coal were the mainsprings of the Nova Scotia economy. So I think what Angus L. decided to do was ward off any possible showdown between the labour movement and Dosco, to defuse industrial warfare in Nova Scotia, by bringing in the trade union act.

The act said that if an employer was already checking off for any purpose—for example, back then companies checked off for coal, for rent, for the church, for the doctor, all these things—then the union could apply and there would be a vote and the employer would have to check-off for the union as well. So after three years of Dosco refusing check-off, the Halifax local walked out.

A delegation of us went to Ottawa. Jim O'Connell, the president of Local 1, met me in Moncton and we went up together. We met with Mackenzie King, Humphrey Mitchell, Pat Conroy—he was secretary-treasurer of the CCL—and A.R. Mosher, the president of the CCL. At that meeting, it was decided that Mackenzie King would put pressure on the province to refer the matter to the Nova Scotia Supreme Court to rule on whether or not Local 1 was eligible to claim its right of check-off under the 1937 act.

We all agreed that the men would go back to work. So the issue went to court. What the company had done, to get itself out from under the law, was on the day that it received the union's letter of request for check-off, it cancelled all the other check-offs it had been making. There was a social club, a medical club, and they used to check-off for coal.

Our local lawyer at the time was R.A. Kanigsberg and we also had J.L. Cohen of Toronto. He came down and he argued before the Supreme Court of Nova Scotia that the 1937 law did apply. He argued that it was just a subterfuge, that it was unreasonable to believe that a company had cancelled all its check-offs without knowing that there was a request from the union for check-off. That was inconceivable, too much of a coincidence.

He argued on that basis before the Supreme Court and he won. So Local 1 got check-off but it was also a big boost for all unions in Nova Scotia because it really put some teeth into the act. Then you could put in your request and you could have check-off. The company couldn't refuse you.

When the Halifax shipyard workers were on strike, by the way, the craft unions tried to slip into the yard to sign a back-door agreement. There was a fellow by the name of Brown—he worked in the naval dockyard next door—and he thought he would pull off a coup and pick up all the shipyard workers for the craft unions during that 1944 strike. He went in and made a deal with the company. He was allowed to go around and organize on company premises while the industrial union representatives were kept out. The craft unions always considered us the upstarts of the labour movement.

* * *

As Local 1 in Halifax and Local 3 in Saint John were direct affiliates of the CCL, they got talking about having a more formal organization. Every two years, there'd be a CCL convention in Ottawa or Toronto and we'd meet with fellows from the west coast and fellows from Quebec. We were hollering to Congress that they should help us form a national union. They said, "No, you're too spread out across the country. It's not economically feasible to form a national union."

The key leaders on the west coast at the time were Malcolm MacLeod and Barry Culhane. Because both of them were from the old country, they had started out in a different way from us. They were an independent craft union. They included the machinists and pipefitters but they didn't belong to the AFL. They were a Canadian, an independent type of group although they eventually became industrialized as time went on. Then Malcolm died of a heart attack and Bill Stewart took over from him, and later on John Fitzpatrick.

Anyway, what Congress finally agreed to was four federations. One in BC, another in Ontario, a third in Quebec and a fourth in the Maritimes. In 1944, we had a couple of meetings in Amherst, Halifax and Saint John. Then we brought in other groups—a local in Pictou, another in Meteghan—and as a result, we set up the Maritime Marine Workers' Council.

A year later, it became the Maritime Marine Workers' Federation. Our founding convention was at the Admiral Beatty Hotel in Saint John. We had about 13 different locals. We became an affiliate of the CCL, not directly chartered as we had been before, which meant that our per capita dues went from being around a dollar per month to about five cents.

I moved to Halifax and became secretary-treasurer of the federation. I think at first I was making around $50 a week, although there was never enough money in the treasury and I'd have to wait. We opened our headquarters in what was known as the Coffin Building, because it was shaped like a coffin, at the foot of Buckingham Street. We shared the office with Local 1. For a while, I think Henry Harm, a Congress representative, worked out of that office too.

Our hope had been that the four federations would eventually come together to form one national union. But what happened is that the yards in Ontario were directly chartered by the CCL and they eventually went with steel. Because Congress was amiss and didn't have bilingual people to service them, the federation in Quebec was engulfed by the Confederation of National Trade Unions, the CNTU. In the Maritimes, Congress tried to push us into steel. We were kind of a free-wheeling type of independent group and they thought that if we went with steel we could be disciplined or controlled.

The leadership of the Marine Workers—myself, Charlie

Murray, Angus MacLeod—always had the reputation of being left-wingers. There was also Milfred Hubley—he was a carpenter in the Dartmouth yard and he became quite active around the end of the war—and Murray Lowe—he became business agent for Local 1 after Charlie Murray. Most of us were from the older generation and we were products of the Depression. We had a different attitude about employers and capitalists. We were much more militant.

If a fellow got fired unfairly, for example, the process of conciliation, of arbitration and negotiating with the company, was long and futile, and we'd say to the fellows, "Why don't you back him up? Walk out." So there'd be a strike for a day or two to get the guy's job back. It was really something to see. If the worker involved had the reputation of being a slacker, however, the men would not take job action on his behalf.

The companies didn't like that. That was considered unreliable, an unstable workforce. The companies would complain to Congress and say, "These guys down here, you know, we can't do business with them. You'll have to do something to get rid of some of these leaders of this local union." The company expected a leadership that would order the men back to work, even if there were unsafe conditions. The media would come up and say to us, "Are you ordering the men back to work?" And we'd say, "No, we're not ordering the men back to work. We're demanding that the government send a man in there and test the darn thing." That was a little bit unorthodox from the way unions were operating.

* * *

The Marine Workers' Federation has always gotten itself into trouble for one reason or another reason. In addition to trying to improve the lot of marine workers, the union also took part in the social issues of the day.

For example, in Saint John, there was a group of people in the south end who were going to be evacuated. Their houses were to be torn down to make way for navy barracks. The union was concerned about what would happen to the people because this was wartime and all the seaport cities were overcrowded. Some of these people came to Angus and me and said, "We need a place to stay. They're tearing down our houses." So we said, "Well, what's City Council doing about it?" They said, "Nothing."

Angus and I went to see Mayor MacKinley. We picked up Frank Crilley and Fred Hodges along the way, and another fellow, John Galbraith from the longshoremen's union, and we told the mayor the problem.

He said, "Well, what can I do about it?"

And we said, "Well, you're the mayor. Use your emergency powers to get them housed somewhere else."

"There's no other housing around," he said.

I thought for a minute, and said, "Yes, there is."

There had been an Ack-Ack [anti-aircraft] troop in east Saint John—during the war they used to protect seaside cities by having guns located around the city—but they had moved them farther out and their buildings were vacant.

I said, "Go in there and take charge of those buildings."

"How?" he said. "You can't go into military buildings."

"Yes, you can. Just take an axe and break the lock."

Galbraith immediately disassociated himself from the group. "Don't include me," he said. "That's too radical for me."

So the mayor called in his secretary and said to me, "Repeat it word-for-word, your advice to me about how to get into those buildings." The secretary didn't know what was going on but I said, "I'm telling the mayor that in view of the housing problem that's been created by the navy building this establishment in the south end of the city and evacuating the residents there, that he should use his emergency powers and if necessary take control of those buildings, even if he has to take an axe and break open the locks." So the secretary wrote all that down and the mayor gave it to the press. The newspaper came out that one member of the delegation seemed to be a very radically-spoken type, Bell.

But this is where we kind of differed from other unions in that we got involved in social issues. It became known around that if you had problems, you could come to the Marine Workers and we'd get involved.

I got myself involved in a similar situation in Halifax. Some of the fellows from the Legion came to see me once. There was supposed to be a housing project for veterans going up around where the Halifax Shopping Centre is now. City Council had promised the whole area for veteran housing but nothing was happening. So they said, "Can you give us a hand?"

At the time, there were two rival newspapers in Halifax, the *Mail* and the *Star*. So I did a little contacting, a little investigation, and I called in the media. I found out that the Halifax Council Committee hadn't met for six months, that four meetings had gone by without a quorum. Two or three of the members on the committee were real estate people. So I came out in the newspapers, charging that the real estate people on the committee—and I named them—were sabotaging the housing project because they wanted to keep the land for themselves.

So first thing I know, I get a subpoena to appear before Judge O. Robertson of Bridgewater. I went to court, me and Gerry McIsaac, and the city solicitor was there. No city councillors, no members of the committee. The judge got me on the stand and said, "This is terrible, impuning their character and their motives. They're good solid citizens." I said, "Well, your honour, I don't think I should apologize. Over half a year has gone by and they haven't been able to convene a meeting. Now if it was for someone else, some big developer, they'd be there on a Sunday. But here it is for a bunch of veterans, and they're not."

So we got into wrangling back and forth and the judge finally said, "Well, have you got any solid proof?" I said, "No, I haven't got any proof. All I wanted was a little action from the committee for them to fulfil their responsibility to have a quorum and do their business." So the next day, it came out in the paper, "Judge Clears City Council." And underneath it said, "Bell admitted to the court that he had no solid evidence but that he was merely trying to activate City Committee into meeting and getting the houses built."

Well, they finally got those houses built. They're along Connaught Avenue but they built them in such a way that the doors wouldn't close. There were places where closets wouldn't close and doors wouldn't open. And that was for veterans of World War II. So we had to get another investigation going.

Jim Bell wrote this poem for the Springhill mining disaster of 1958:

Springhill 1958

Dig deep, you blackened sons of toil,
Black gold is dug, not raised in sun-drenched soil.
Dig deep, the hell is near and 'tis dark and damp,
The devil loves oil, but he'll steal your lamp.

Have you ridden the rake to the level below,
And clawed at the face of the ebony coal?
Can you set the rate of datal pay
For a human mole by the hour or day?
How many boxes do the miners fill,
Before the bumping pit, a worker kills?

Sleep, in your undug grave 'neath rock and coal,
You've added to the coffers and are tallied in the toll,
And what do you bequeath to the milling pithead crowd?
Your place, your pan, your broken lamp, but not your shroud.

J.K. Bell
Halifax, Nova Scotia

CHAPTER SIX

Purged!

As soon as I moved to Halifax, Milfred Hubley and I, and several other people, formed a CCL Council in the city. It was very small and very insignificant compared to the Trades and Labour Council (TLC) in Halifax. The CCL federation was strong provincially—it was dominated by the miners and steelworkers—although we were weak in Halifax. There, we had only a dozen locals, a few CBRT locals, the brewery workers, the shipyard workers. The TLC federation was the reverse—strong in Halifax and weak provincially.

We set up a joint committee of the CCL and TLC in Halifax. It was called the Halifax Joint Labour Educational Committee. It came about because of the efforts of a German professor at Dalhousie University, a Dr. Richter. He thought that labour should be involved in the educational process so he called in various labour groups, the CCL, the TLC, even some people who weren't affiliated to either. The purpose of the committee was to educate people about unions. He later got killed in a bicycle accident and Guy Henson, who was his assistant, took over.

At the time, the CCL and the TLC people in Ottawa weren't on good terms. We had a few get-togethers—one at Dalhousie University, others at the vocational school in Halifax—and neither the TLC or the CCL people from Ottawa wanted to come. They were afraid that the workers in Halifax were up to something. But each group was invited and each was afraid that the other would come so, in the end, both of them came down.

There were only a couple other joint labour councils in

Canada, like ours, that had defied the TLC and CCL about not meeting together. There was a movement across Canada where labour councils were beginning to merge. This was long before the national bodies would merge. [In 1956, the CCL and the TLC merged to become the Canadian Labour Congress—the CLC. A similar merger was formalized in the US between the AFL and CIO.]

* * *

In November, 1956, the Nova Scotia Federation of Labor (TLC) and the Nova Scotia Provincial Federation of Labor (CCL) followed the lead of their respective organizations on the national level (which had merged in April to form the Canadian Labor Congress) to form one provincial Federation of Labor. The newly-elected president was Ben O'Neil and secretary-treasurer was Hugh MacLeod.

The following appeared in the Halifax Chronicle Herald:

Nova Scotia's organized labor formed its new parliament in Halifax Tuesday, decided to ban from membership any organization controlled by non-democratic elements, and voted itself the power to refuse a seat in convention to any individual espousing Communism, Fascism or other totalitarianism.

And in so doing, the new Federation of Labor caused a sharp encounter in the first day of its inaugural convention which jammed the auditorium of the Seagull Club in Halifax.

Key figures in the debate were Sinclair Allen, a Halifax trolley coach operator who as chairman of a committee steered through the new constitution; Ben O'Neil, of the Sydney Steelworkers Union, who supported the writing-in of the anti-Communist clauses, and James K. Bell, a member of the Halifax marine union who charged the action to ban individuals was "contrary to the constitution of the parent Canadian Labor Congress...and endangered the autonomy of local unions affiliated with the provincial body...

"In Canada," he said, "there is a new Canadian Labor Congress, and views of this national body were plainly set out in April. There is a basic principle involved here. As long as an organization pays its per capita tax it can send any delegate it chooses to the federation convention."

He followed: "It takes all types of people to make up a local union. And in taking all workers in, there are bound to be people who have views not approved by the majority. But in passing this passage you are endangering the autonomy of affiliated organizations."

Mr. Bell told the delegates there are fascists in Canada "who were brought here from Europe with government assistance. There are storm troopers too. Let's not kid ourselves.

"I find this unconstitutional. This federation is challenging the constitution of the parent federation."

When the matter came to a vote, Mr. Bell cast the only "nay vote" in the convention attended by 180 delegates.

One of my good friends during this time was Tom McLachlan, the son of old J.B. McLachlan, probably one of Cape Breton's most famous labour leaders. Tom later became president of District 26 of the United Mine Workers in Cape Breton and also president of the CCF in Nova Scotia. Tom was a left-winger, like myself. A lot of times we'd go to a Congress convention and questions would come up, for example, about recognition of China, and we'd get up and speak in favour.

Well, that was very bad, you know. To recognize China? We believed that you couldn't leave out a quarter of the people on the earth. You couldn't just ignore them. But to recognize China—for most of the labour movement that was subversive. I remember I was on the floor and they stopped the convention. A.R. [Mosher] was in the chair and he ordered them to cut the mike. And I still hollered that I thought Congress was wrong, that Congress should recognize China as a country we should be dealing with.

There was a lot of red-baiting at the Congress level in those days. In the US, they had brought in the Taft–Hartley Act that said that you couldn't hold a position in a union, couldn't be a leader if you were also a communist. The Congress executive reworded that so that you had to take an oath. If you were a candidate for a Congress office, you had to swear that you would uphold the democratic institutions of Canada. This was passed at a convention in 1948. I got up and spoke against it. As far as I was concerned, communists had done too much for the trade union movement to be barred from it.

Congress had begun to see communists everywhere. There was a phobia, you know. It was the McCarthy era and the country was being whipped up into a hysteria. I had been a vice-president of the Nova Scotia Federation of Labour (CCL) for a couple of years, but then the word came down from Ottawa to purge the communists from the labour movement in Nova Scotia.

* * *

The Federation convention in 1949 was held at the Firemen's Parlour in Glace Bay. The night before it started, I was drinking with John R. "Daw" MacDonald when his brother, Angus "Blue," knocked on the hotel door. Angus "Blue" was a colourful

J.K. Bell was an avid letter writer.

MARITIME MARINE WORKERS' FEDERATION

521 Barrington Street,

HALIFAX, N. S.

Phone 3-6039

PRESIDENT
HARRY A. TAYLOR

VICE-PRESIDENT
HAROLD SCOTT

SECRETARY-TREASURER
J K. BELL

EXECUTIVE MEMBERS
MILFRED HUBLEY
WILLIAM EMMERICH
GERALD LYNCH

Affiliated to the Canadian Congress of Labour.

Representing the Majority of Organized Marine and Shipbuilding Workers in the Maritimes.

December 18, 1945.

Rt. Hon. J. L. McKenzie King,
Prime Minister,
Ottawa, Ontario.

Honorable Sir:

This organization strongly protests the sale of Canadian surplus war material through the Dutch Netherlands government, to be used against the Indonesian people in their fight for independence.

It is our opinion that any credits extended to European governments should be used to re-habilitate the people of Europe and not to help finance Colonial wars. This protest has the endorsation of a large section of the working people in this country and your government should act to prevent any further war surpluses being sold to those countries who would use such surpluses as an instrument of re-action either within their home territories or in their colonies.

> I remain,
> Yours very truly,
> J.K. Bell
> Secretary-Treasurer

JKB:EW

*   *   *

Dec. 29th, 1947

Hon. J.L. Mackenzie King,
Prime Minister,
Ottawa, Ont.

Hon. sir:

On behalf of Maritime shipyard workers strong protest is being registered over the sale of arms and munitions to the anti-democratic Chinese warlords. Canada's intervention in the Chinese civil war can be compared as 'legalized gun running' which by no means can be looked upon with decency and respect.

If your government could not see fit to assist the Spanish people against fascist France it ill behooves the present actions of your government in assisting France's counterpart in China. Or is all this the real indication of your governments' policies at home and abroad.

In the interests of peace and democracy we urge your government to prohibit the further shipment of arms and munitions to China.

> Yours truly,
> J.K. Bell
> Secretary-Treas.

Cape Breton labour man. He was on the Glace Bay Town Council and the Cape Breton Labour Council. The right wing had sent him round to find out what was going on. They were afraid that John R. might come over with Tom and me and support us during elections the next day.

So Angus "Blue" comes in, sees we're having a drink and swings around. "Oh, you're a bunch of drunks." He goes out. So John said, "Be careful. Angus has been picked as the guy who's taking you on. He's gonna criticize you to the fullest."

What had happened, just before the convention, a fellow got killed in the coal mines and he was from out west. So Tom had called me up to see if we could find some money to ship his body home. The Workmen's Compensation Act permitted only $50 at the time to transport a body. And Tom said, "We haven't got the money." They had tried to take up a collection at the pit head but it didn't pan out. Angus "Blue" had volunteered to deliver the body but everybody figured he just wanted a free trip out west.

I had gone down to see the head of the Workmen's Compensation Board to see if we could get special dispensation. The government had agreed to increase the $50 somewhat. So I had written up a report that I presented to the convention. After I sat down, Angus "Blue" tackled me. "I don't agree with Brother Bell," he said, "or with Angus L. or the chairman of the Compensation Board. Furthermore, Brother Bell ain't explaining it right. For example, you take a dead man living in Glace Bay and he wants to go west. I maintain, Brother Chairman, that that fella can go as far west as he wants and can take whoever he wants with him." He was obviously referring to himself but he was also arguing that we were getting too soft with government. So that was my defeat.

Of course, I would have lost anyway. It was in the cards for the left wing because Freeman Jenkins—he was president of the Mine Workers then, a right-winger—he had been contacted by the CCL in Ottawa to take in a delegation of miners who were supporters of his. So he took in a bunch, there was a heavy representation by miners and they cleaned us out. I was beaten by John Lynk. Milfred Hubley lost as well, although John R. "Daw" managed to stay on.

* * *

Above: *A break in proceedings at the CCL convention in Toronto in 1954 gives delegates a chance to socialize. Jim Bell is third from left. To his left is longtime companion Alice Dickey, who died in 1991.*

Below: *The founding meeting of the Maritime Marine Workers' Council, later the Marine Workers' Federation, was held at the Nova Scotia Hotel in Halifax in 1944. Jim Bell (front row, second from right) went to work full-time for the federation once it was formed. Angus MacLeod is shown front row, centre. The issue of the day, as the background banner shows, was the 40-hour work week.*

A lot of fellows who ran for office and who got rejected by the federation didn't bother to go to conventions after that. But I went to every convention. I'd run for a position every year just to let the delegates know I was there and I'd get defeated. [Jim did not get re-elected to the Nova Scotia Federation of Labour executive until 1965.] What the hell. I read Abraham Lincoln's life story one time. He ran nine times before he got elected to a county position.

There was this guy, Tom Mombourquette, who was a vice-president of the federation. He used to kid me a lot. He'd say, "Jesus, I'd be radical, too, if I was in your position. You're getting paid by the Marine Workers, you're getting paid by the Communist Party of Canada and you're also getting paid by the Comintern in Moscow."

"Well," I said, "I'll tell you what, Tom. I'll make you my agent. Now if I'm entitled to a salary from the Communist Party of Canada or the Comintern, you collect it. I'll sign you power of attorney, and I'll give you 25 percent." That was the kind of propaganda that they used to spread around at election times.

I remember one time at a convention in Kentville, I ran and they got into a squabble over what colour of ballot to use. They had a book of coloured ballots. So I said, "Let's simplify this. Let's use the red ballots." They all got a chuckle out of that.

Another time at a national convention, I ran against Donnie MacDonald. This was in 1972. He was one of the main guys in Congress who'd been trying to keep me out of the labour movement over the years and I was mad at him. I held him responsible for the trouble I was getting in Nova Scotia. So I said, "To hell with him. I'm not going to give him the honour of going in by acclamation." Someone said, "I nominate J.K. Bell" to run as president and I said, "I accept." I got almost 400 votes compared to his 650. That kind of upset Donnie quite badly. He couldn't figure out how a commie who had no campaign could do so well. That kind of increased the intensity of his dislike for me and the Marine Workers after that.

Donnie MacDonald was born in Halifax, like me. His father used to be on the Dosco ships but he died. So when his mother became a widow, she moved the family to Sydney. Donnie went to St. Francis Xavier for a while and he came out and there were no decent jobs around so he went to work shovelling coal onto the ships at the coal pier in Whitney Pier. He became president of the United Mine Workers local there and they had a griev-ance—probably a rightful grievance—and Donnie called them out on a wildcat. The UMW contract with Dosco apparently had a clause that said the employer could fire a person for calling a wildcat strike so they fired Donnie.

So then he got a job as manager of the co-op store that had just got organized and from the co-op he went and ran for the CCF and got elected. For a short time, he was even Leader of the Opposition in Nova Scotia. All this took place in a matter of a couple of years. First thing you know, he was in the legislature as an MLA. After that, he went to work for the CCL. He was just an ordinary CCL representative before he became director of organization. I had assisted him in a number of organizing attempts, Moir's Chocolates in Halifax, the veneer plant in Saint John, things like that. We got along okay until one night at the Lord Elgin Hotel when we were at a Congress convention in Ottawa. Milfred Hubley and I were staying at a tourist home. It was a dollar a night, bed and breakfast. And Donnie had a big room at the Lord Elgin.

So we went up to his room to see him. He was drinking and we had a drink off him. He started in on us. "Why do you always stay in flop houses, Bell? Why don't you stay in a hotel?" I said, "We can't afford it. We're all right. It's a good place." But he kept on. So I said, "Lookit, MacDonald, here you are, all dressed up with a suit and gold cuff links and playing the part of a duke"— that's what they called him, Donnie the Duke, behind his back—"you're so far removed from the working man that they wouldn't recognize you or you wouldn't recognize them." Well, he got right mad at that. He practically started crying. After that, we were more or less critics of each other.

* * *

At one time, there were CIA agents running around the hall at Congress conventions and they were given credentials or observer status. They were going around with the right-wingers and they were saying, "Who's that fellow and what's his connection?" And they would go back and prepare a dossier. They were connected to the American Embassy as attachés.

A number of them sent me little notes. "Come up into my room. I'd like to have a talk with you." I'd ignore them because I knew who they were. They wanted to get you into their room and provoke you into an argument and have you say things. They'd have their recorders there and they'd get it all down. So I wouldn't bother. Then they'd send photographers around. "Take this guy's picture." On several occasions, it was raised at the convention, "Who are these people?" but the reaction would just be, "They're guests," or something like that. Some of the left-wingers would get up and say, "We don't want any more of these CIA spies in here, taking our pictures and recording our statements."

As far as the Congress went, I always took the position that I had my views and they had theirs. Being labelled a communist certainly stopped me from advancing in the labour movement. I could have perhaps gone a lot farther. I've seen a lot of fellows work their way up in the labour movement, but that sort of thing didn't appeal to me if it meant having to hide my views. I suppose the fact that I didn't have a family gave me another degree of independence. I just spoke and said how I felt.

I never aspired to be president of the Nova Scotia Federation of Labour. And even if I was a first officer or not, I still had a role. You know, you learn the same lesson at the head of the class as you do at the foot. Even outside the executive, I used to make my views known to the politicians and to the media as to what labour wanted.

The strange thing about our relationship with Congress was that, although they didn't like the Marine Workers' Federation, every time they needed a staff person or a representative from the Atlantic region, they selected him from our union. Pat Shea, Henry Harm, Bill Craig, Angus MacLeod, Ralph Spragg—they all went on Congress staff. When they needed a full-time guy to organize and deal with employers down here, they came to us. But officially, they viewed us as renegades.

CHAPTER SEVEN

A Merchant Marine
and the CSU

We first got to know the Canadian Seamen's Union in Saint John. Local 3 had an office and a large meeting hall that we were using only about once or twice a month. So we rented it occasionally to them. The CSU had begun in 1936, originally set up to organize seamen on the Great Lakes. For a while, it was affiliated with the Seafarer's International Union, which was an AFL union, although it eventually broke away. When the war began, the CSU moved into organizing men on the deepsea vessels.

We always supported the Canadian Seamen's Union because they were an industrial and a Canadian union, like us, and they were militants. Of course, a lot of the CSU leadership would have been considered communist. Pat Sullivan and Dewar Ferguson, for example. Sullivan was the president and Ferguson was elected to the Toronto City Council as a Labor-Progressive Party candidate. Both were openly communist. Also Charlie Murray, who organized fishermen in Nova Scotia for the CSU before the war.

The guy in charge of the CSU organization in Halifax was Bert Meade. He and his wife Ethel came here from the US where they had been connected with the NMU—the National Maritime Union—on the river and lake boats. The CSU fellows would not stay long as business agent or port agent because they had gone to sea for adventure and to make money. The port agent wouldn't make as much as the fellows on the ships with their overtime and they wouldn't have the same excitement as the guys travelling around the world. So guys would stay in the job for two or three months and do the paperwork but then they would give it up. There was a constant turnover of fellows.

So Bert Meade came to Halifax and Jack Shaw came down from Montreal. Those two stayed for a reasonable time as port agents. Bert was a large man, not a hard fellow to get along with. The only thing was that he had a style about him sometimes— kind of an American style—and some of the boys used to resent it. He was quite formal. He would make an appointment, for example, where the other fellows didn't do such things. You saw them when you saw them. But Bert wasn't a bad head when you got to know him. He came in just after the CSU had organized the ferry workers in Halifax, who we later took in with us.

The CSU also set up two other organizations, the Canadian Fish Handlers' Union and the Canadian Fishermen's Union. The fellows that worked aboard the fishing vessels and the fellows who worked in the plants were chartered separately by the CSU. Meade negotiated the first contracts with National Sea Products.

We supported the CSU because they supported us in demanding that Canadian vessels not only be manned by Canadians but be built by Canadians. The SIU always said that they didn't care where ships were built as long as they had the right to man them. Once we got the Marine Workers' Federation going in 1945, one of our first big campaigns was to have a Canadian Merchant Marine.

Canada had had a merchant marine in the post-war period after World War I. It was called the CGMM—the Canadian Government Merchant Marine. During World War II, the government built a tremendous number of vessels—they called them the Parks vessels because they were all named after national parks—and it set up the Park Steamship Company to operate them. These vessels were all steam-powered. The CSU had even signed a collective agreement during the war with a number of operators who leased these vessels.

But by the end of the war, the Parks vessels were an outdated class that couldn't compete with the diesel vessels coming out in different countries. We suggested that Canada should replace them with modern, up-to-date vessels so that Canada could retain her position as a world trader.

Shipping immediately picked up after the war and there was

a great need for vessels. But philosophically, the Liberal government of the day was opposed to that. Great Britain had been
making noises that their balance of trade was unfair with
Canada, that we weren't providing them with an opportunity to
make money. So the Canadian government took the position
that Britain should be encouraged as a shipping nation, and that
we should hand the shipping monopoly to Great Britain as a way
of allowing them to make foreign currency.

That's not what happened, of course. These vessels were
originally leased by Canadian operators on condition that they
were kept under Canadian registry. But the shipping companies
hired W.J. Fisher as their representative and he got after the
government to allow them to put the vessels under foreign
registry and from there to sell them. The money was supposed to
go into an escrow account to build up Canada's merchant
marine. But what the companies did instead was use the money
to build a new fleet of lakers.

The outdated lakers were replaced but not the deepsea vessels. We were saying, "Lookit, most of these lakers are being built
either in the United States or Upper Canada. We're getting very
few. Practically none were being built in the Atlantic region."

What we wanted was a foreign deepsea fleet of diesel vessels
with the latest technology. It would have meant a lot of work for
our members and it would have given Canada a deepsea fleet for
naval purposes. But the Great Lakes got built up reasonably well
with Canadian vessels, but not the merchant marine. So the
result of the government's policy was to destroy the shipbuilding
industry in Canada as we knew it.

* * *

The Seafarer's International Union was brought into Canada
with the connivance of government for the very purpose of
scuttling the CSU. Basically, it was because the CSU was
becoming more and more militant every year and demanding
more and better conditions from the employers.

What government wanted was to create a scenario that would
show that it was impossible for Canadian ship owners to operate
these ships, and at the same time, to give labour a black eye.
They wanted to show that unions were so unreliable that the

members were fighting among themselves. That would give the operators a chance to say, "We can't operate with all the economic problems we have now, with all the union problems we have. We have to get out of this whole mess. You have to allow us to sell these vessels off."

Government officials went down to see the SIU in the US and encouraged them to send up some fellows to start a union war with the CSU. It came out later that Milton Gregg, the federal minister of labour at the time—he was originally from New Brunswick—actually went out to California and interviewed the head of the Sailors' Union of the Pacific, which was associated with the SIU. He wanted them to spare a man to come up and chase the CSU out of the Great Lakes and the deepsea.

As soon as the SIU came into Canada, the CCL gave them shelter. They had an ally in the railway union named Frank Hall and he was a right-winger. He was so deathly scared of anyone left of centre that he would gladly see a gangster at the head of a union than someone with a socialist ideology. He more or less took Hal Banks [head of the SIU] under his wing. What the SIU did was create fights between themselves and the CSU and this led to a lot of publicity and gave some credence to the owners' argument that they were finding it difficult to operate because of the union rivalry that was going on.

The labour movement knew that the Liberal government of the day was playing ball with the American gangster union in order to set up a scenario that two unions were fighting in Canada. But actually it wasn't two unions in Canada—one was an imported union with a lot of thugs brought in from the States.

In those days, the establishment—the government and business and even some elements of the labour movement—would align itself with a corrupt union rather than a good, fairly administered union if that union was considered left wing. A union that came out openly as anti-communist was acceptable even if it was corrupt. At that particular time, I remember Al Capone in Chicago making a speech before one of the Chicago boards of trade, that we have to protect our youth from the evils of communism, that they're poisoning the minds of the youth of America. The fact that he was shooting them down, selling

The 4th annual convention of the Marine Workers' Federation was held in Saint John, N.B. in July 1949. Jim was still on crutches as a result of being run down in Montreal by Hal Banks's goons the preceding fall.

them drugs, or getting them involved in prostitution, that was all acceptable. As long as you were anti-communist.

* * *

I remember being at a CCL convention in Ottawa in October of 1948. There was supposed to be a meeting of support for the CSU in Montreal afterwards so I was going to stop in. I was warned in Ottawa not to go. Some people said, "Look, if you're going to attend that meeting supporting the CSU, you better not because the SIU people will get you." I never paid much attention to them.

I went to Montreal and I went to the meeting. There were around 15 or 20 people there. Coming out of the meeting, I was going across the street when this car came down the street with its lights off and it struck me. I went up into the air and landed on the hood of the car and went through the windshield. The driver of the car panicked and swerved the car towards the sidewalk. There were two guys in the car and they jumped out and took off.

Other people coming out of the meeting found me on the hood of the car with my face through the windshield and they called an ambulance. I went to the Royal Victoria Hospital in Montreal. This was late October and I was in the hospital until the end of the year. Around Christmas time, this heavy-set man came in and brought me a bag of candy and a few other things. He said, "You don't know me and I don't know you. Another fellow in the labour movement sent me up here with a little message. His name is Harry Bridges [head of the International Longshoremen's and Warehousemen's Union]. He said, 'You know that guy that made you suffer, well, he is suffering too.'" That was all he said and he turned around and walked out.

So I assumed that the longshoremen's union had found out who ran me down and did the same to him. I assumed that it had been one of Hal Banks's goons.

My leg was broken in 14 places and after I got out of the hospital, I was on crutches for a year and a half. I think that if that hadn't happened, I would have been able to mobilize some shipyard workers to be on the docks during the CSU strike in Halifax in April 1949.

The CSU was on strike and the SIU had been making a drive to take over their ships. There were a couple of places abroad that the shipowners were able to replace the crews in foreign ports with the help of foreign police. But up until that point, they hadn't been able to displace a Canadian crew in a Canadian port. What they were planning on doing was pulling it off either in Saint John or Halifax. By putting me in the hospital, I wasn't on the scene to help mobilize supporters to go down with the CSU boys. They used to depend on us to a fair extent to organize support in the shipyards.

The SIU brought their goons from Montreal to Truro, and then put them in a railway box car to Halifax. The railway car was allowed to cross the picket line to get into the yard. When they opened the doors, the SIU goons came out with clubs. Some of them had sawed-off shotguns and once they took over the ship they fired on the CSU guys. About eight of the pickets were severely injured.

After that, the CSU was beaten. CSU-manned ships were strike-bound in different ports throughout the world, and one by one their picket lines were broken and their crews replaced by SIU members. The Halifax incident was the CSU's last strike. The union eventually lost its bargaining rights. The steamship companies signed a contract on the Great Lakes with the SIU and eventually the few ships that were still deepsea, they signed up with the SIU too. And that was basically the end of the CSU.

CHAPTER EIGHT
1950s: Canadian Supreme Court Decision on Communists

In 1951, the Marine Workers' Federation had organized locals at shipyards in Dartmouth, Lunenburg, Pictou and Liverpool. So, being secretary-treasurer, I was the one who signed the application for certification with the Nova Scotia Labour Relations Board. The application was opposed by the Smith and Rhuland yard in Lunenburg because of the fact that I was supposedly a communist.

I remember going to visit the local in that yard in Lunenburg. That's the yard where they built the *Bluenose*. It was a wooden boatyard. Bob Winters, the cabinet minister for the area, had an office in the same building where we had the union office. He came in and addressed the guys when I wasn't there and told them that they were making a grave mistake in belonging to a union that Bell was connected with. To their credit, they rejected his advice and stayed in the union. They were with the union right up until that yard closed. There were probably about 100 guys there at the time.

So the issue went before the Nova Scotia Labour Relations Board. Horace Read was the chairman and J.P. Bell was the chief executive. There were two labour representatives on the board— Sydney Oram who was with the mine workers and Jim Dwyer with the carpenters' union. The board denied the certification. They said that to certify a union with me in the leadership would "confer power to persons who would use those powers primarily to advance communist policies."

Syd Oram was president of the Nova Scotia Federation of Labour at the time. He told me in New Glasgow that he voted against the decision. Jimmy Dwyer, too. He met me on a number of occasions and said, "Don't worry about me, Jim, I did right." But when our lawyer asked J.P. Bell how each member voted, he hedged but admitted that it was unanimous. So we were sold out by our two brothers on the board.

Not only was the certification denied in Lunenburg but also in Pictou, Dartmouth and Liverpool. So we took it to the Nova Scotia Supreme Court. They decided that the board had made an error in law, that the board didn't have a right to throw out a certification on that basis. But then Smith and Rhuland appealed that decision to the Supreme Court of Canada.

By this time, the CCL was supporting us. They were supporting the principle that politics shouldn't stop you from being able to sign a certification order. So they hired a lawyer—his name was Wright—and they went before the Supreme Court of Canada with us. Our lawyers were Kanigsberg and MacKeigan.

The Supreme Court upheld the decision of the Nova Scotia court. It pointed out that there was no law in the country against holding communist views or being a member of a group or party supporting them, so you couldn't exclude someone from a trade union on that basis. That was a major decision for the Marine Workers, not just for me, because in every local there was someone considered to be left wing—Angus MacLeod in Saint John, Milfred Hubley in Dartmouth. So bit by bit, they would have been able to decertify the locals. It would have removed the leadership, and the workers may have been discouraged and left too.

But that decision didn't come down until 1953 and by then the Pictou yard had been turned over to the United Steelworkers. We had organized the Pictou yard during the war. But then the yard went flat and the union kind of folded up, although there was still a charter. When the yard was revived again in the early 1950s, we went in and signed up the workers, and we had to go through the certification process again.

While we were in the process of getting certification—along with the certifications in Lunenburg, Dartmouth, and Liverpool—the company in Pictou fired the local executive in the yard. So we recommended job action and the men all walked out in support. While they were out, the steelworkers went in and signed a back-door agreement with the company. The steelworkers signed the contract without any members. You can't do that today. The laws are different now. So gradually the men all decided to go in and sign up with the steelworkers so they could go back to work.

We complained to Congress and they ordered the steelworkers to return the local to us, but they refused. They were a big union and powerful and they just defied Congress. So the Pictou yard has been a steelworkers local ever since.

After that, we went before Angus L. one time and I said, "Mr. Premier, I think the labour laws should be clarified as to whether or not a person's religious or political beliefs should affect the determination of the Labour Relations Board in matters of certification." And he said, "Well now, you raise an interesting point, Bell. For the record, tell me, are you or are you not a communist?"

And I said, "Why do you ask that question, Mr. Premier? Your board has already judged me to be one and you appear to be in support of the board's action so you've obviously judged me to be one. Are you in doubt?"

"Well," he said, "I'm not taking any of that nonsense from any of you communists."

For a while, I thought he was ready to punch me in the face.

* * *

Another sore spot between us and Congress was that we always maintained a relationship with the Quebec federation of shipyard workers even though it wasn't part of the CCL or CLC. We always had fraternal delegates back and forth and Congress didn't like that. At one point, we put out a policy on shipbuilding in French and English sponsored by the three federations—the west coast, Quebec and the Maritimes. Congress felt that nothing should be taken up with Ottawa unless it went through them. That kind of got us in hot water with Congress, that we were operating outside their influence.

I remember one time I was in Quebec City at CNTU headquarters at 999 Charest Boulevard. Who was there but Pierre Trudeau and Jean Marchand. This would have been in the 1950s, before Trudeau got involved in politics. So we were discussing social problems and Trudeau started giving me a lecture. "You know, Bell," he said, "you don't want to waffle on these things. You've got to take a stand. You've got to come out for the workers and shake up the establishment."

At that time, the companies were doing everything but trying to put me in jail so I don't know if he knew to what extent I was tagged and labelled down here.

The next thing I knew, Gerard Pelletier, Marchand and Trudeau had joined the Liberal Party. This was around the time we had set up a joint labour committee in Halifax, so I suggested bringing Pelletier down to Halifax to our conference at Dalhousie University. He was a short man and he wore one of these black berets. He came down and he gave a sort of left wing address.

After that, Trudeau arrived in Saint John as Prime Minister. He was met by the MP for Saint John, fellow by the name of Riley, and Riley took him down to see Frank Crilley. Frank was kind of a left wing gadfly, a nice fellow. He was a poet and well-read. His father had wanted him to go into the priesthood but instead Frank became the town radical. He was a good friend of mine. When I was in Saint John, Frank and I would always get together and discuss things.

When he met Trudeau, he said, "I have a bit of a memo here with your name on it." And Frank went over to the drawer and took out the receipt of a donation he had made to the asbestos strike in Quebec. The asbestos workers had been on strike and Trudeau at the time was a technical advisor and in charge of fundraising for the strike. So Trudeau was quite enthralled by that. So then, Trudeau came to Halifax and Gerry Regan was taking him to the north end community centre. The union office was just a stone's throw away and Gerry stopped the car. It was a rainy day and he came in and got me to come out. He introduced me and we shook hands by the car and Trudeau said, "You look kind of familiar." And I said, "Yeah, we met in Quebec."

* * *

After Angus L. died, the interim premier was Harold Connolly. One time we were in before the government—there was usually quite a crowd of us at these meetings, about 40 or 50—and the president of the steelworkers union in Sydney, Martin Merner, was at the back of the hall. Once the presentation was finished, I said, "Mr. Premier, can I make a suggestion?" And he said,

"What's that, Bell?" I said, "Well, a lot of our people are finding it difficult to go to Montreal for cobalt treatment. Why can't we have a cobalt bomb here in the Atlantic region."

Well, "bomb" caught the ear of Merner, and he said to the guys around him, "Listen to that. We've got to keep that Bell the hell out of these delegations. The son of a bitch is crazy. He's got bombs on the brain. All he thinks about is bombs and guns and revolution."

So Connolly said, "Well, by coincidence, a representative of the Atomic Energy Commission has been in to see me this week and we're interested in buying one for the Victoria General Hospital."

I said, "I understand that the cobalt bomb only costs $65,000." And he said, "Well, there's more expense to it than that."

Anyway, we were discussing this and Don Nicholson, the president of the CBRT&GW, and some others are laughing their heads off at the back of the room at Merner for saying all I think about is bombs.

* * *

We got to know Gerald Regan around the time of the gypsum strike in Windsor in 1958. He was just a young fellow at the time, not long out of law school, and he had been hired to represent gypsum workers in their strike with Canadian Gypsum. Tom Shires was president, and myself, Hugh J. MacLeod, Henry Harm, Sinclair Allen, Don Nicholson, among others, were helping out. That was a bitter strike and after it was over, the Marine Workers hired Regan. We put him on a retainer.

Because we had him on a retainer, the guys in the yard just assumed he was there for them. I remember one time one of the fellows in the yard got arrested for having mash in his house. A mountie arrested him on a Friday but it was a long weekend and he made the fatal mistake of not getting the mash tested in the lab until Tuesday morning. Regan had noted it in the police report.

Vincent Pottier was the judge at the time and Regan said, "We're not contesting the fact that my client owns the mash. What we're contesting is that when my client owned it, it was legal. It became illegal in the custody of the Mounted Police.

When was that mash tested?" The mountie was all embarrassed and he had to admit that it wasn't tested until Tuesday morning. So the judge said, "I've got to give you the benefit of the doubt. Case dismissed."

Another time, one of the guys got arrested for speeding out near the Halifax airport, where the road coming into Dartmouth joins the road coming into Halifax at Miller Lake. Regan happened to go by there and he noticed there was a big transformer. He had read somewhere that radar was not accurate when used around a transformer. So he brought this out during the trial.

He had the mountie on the stand and he asked him, "Do you know how radar works?" And the fellow had to admit that he didn't know much about it. And Regan said to the judge, "Your Honour, I contend that radar was not accurate by virtue of the fact that the transformer was there." So the judge took a recess and checked it out and I guess there is an effect by transformers on radar. So the judge threw it out. "I've got to give this man the benefit of the doubt," he said.

The boys in the yard thought that any time they got in trouble, Regan was already being paid by the union. So they never paid him. Regan and I often laughed about it afterwards. We just gave him a few hundred dollars retainer a year. He carried on as our lawyer even after he became an MP.

* * *

Gerald Regan and [NDP leader] Jeremy Akerman used to come to the Marine Workers' club on Gerrish Street. That's where they met. I introduced them to each other. See, during the war, the employers, the elite in Halifax had private clubs. Liquor was rationed then and members would leave their ration books at the club so that someone from the club would go out and buy theirs. We used that as an excuse to get a club going ourselves. We said, "What about the working class?" We went before the government and said, "By the time our shipyard workers get a chance to go to the liquor store on Saturday, all the booze is gone."

So they gave us the right to have clubs in Saint John, Dartmouth, and Halifax. The club in Halifax was on the corner of Agricola and North. It was upstairs in a building just next to the Oddfellows Hall. We used to use the Oddfellows Hall sometimes for a meeting. Then we moved down and bought the building on Gerrish Street. That was the Marine Workers' Federation headquarters and the club was upstairs. It was called the Shipyard Club. Bomber Forbes was the bartender.

Bomber was a former SIU member. He'd sailed around the world on ships when he was a teenager. He was working in the pipefitting department at the shipyards and he came out of the yards to run the club.

At first you had to leave your ration book at the club and the club steward would buy a quart of liquor or beer in your name. Your name was on your bottle and you were only supposed to drink your own bottle. In effect what it did was prevent you from bringing a friend to the club for a drink. But the elite, the upper class, it was common knowledge that, at their club, they could take a friend in and have a drink, and they didn't have to account for every drink. We were treated more like children.

So Milfred Hubley and I and several others formed the Nova Scotia Association of Social Clubs. We used to go before government for reform of the Liquor Commission. We'd make representations to the chairman of the Liquor Licensing Board that was headed up by Judge Crowell. We said, "Why don't you just allow us a quota for the club based on membership size."

All these guys—Gerry Regan, Doug Harkness, Frank Miller, Harry Flemming—they all used to come to our club. RCMP guys used to come too. We'd get a couple of drinks in us and Doug Harkness—he was a television broadcaster from Amherst—he'd say, "What strikes are you pulling off in the near future?" And there'd be a couple of these guys from intelligence sitting near us and I'd say, "Well, we just had the strike with this particular company and we're looking at picking on that other capitalist so and so. We'll pull a strike on him pretty soon." And they'd be sitting there and looking at each other. Harkness could identify them and so could I.

The first Press Club started in the Canadian Pacific building on Granville Street. So the first thing, they came to me and said, "We're giving you the right to belong to the Press Club." I think it was $50 or so to join. So I said, "Okay," and I split my drinking between our club and the Press Club.

So then they moved to the lower rooms of the Carleton Hotel and we used to go up there. The Legislative Assembly would sit on Monday evenings—they'd have a night session to give the MLAs a chance to drive in from around the province during the day—and after the session, they'd all come up to the Press Club.

I always had a lot more trouble among labour people than I ever did with politicians and business people, about all this red stuff.

CHAPTER NINE
1961 Strike

As I said earlier, the dry dock in Saint John was owned by C.N. Wilson and F.M. Ross. After the war, there were lean times in the yards and Wilson thought up the bright scheme of putting some of the men on salary. He said that he had no money to pay for overtime. So he offered them a deal although not to everyone, just to certain people, mainly people who had been vocal in the union. He would give them a weekly salary with no overtime. They were called the "88." That's the number of people that he wanted to be on salary.

That almost split the union. Some of the guys were for it. Some weren't. One guy would be called in for a rush job and he'd be paid by the hour. The fellow next to him would be paid by the week. A repair job would come in that the "88" was not supposed to touch until the people in the street were hired. But they would go down and do it. A fellow would say, "Somebody told me you used an acetylene torch and you were doing some cutting while I'm out here on welfare, on the street. And I agreed that you could be an 88'er." So it caused a lot of friction.

After Ross left to go out west, Wilson had wanted to pull out of the dry dock. He had two sons but neither was interested in running it so, in the late 1950s, Wilson decided to sell the dry dock to K.C. Irving. Irving had built a refinery but he needed an outlet to the waterfront. It had been called Saint John Dry Dock and Shipbuilding Company but after Irving bought it, he called it the Saint John Shipbuilding and Dry Dock Company although it was basically the same operation. He also bought the Saint John Ironworks, the Saint John Tugboat Company, and there were three or four others. All these companies had been owned by Wilson and Ross.

Wilson had done well with the yard and with his other businesses. He was certainly not a poor man, although he didn't get a very big price when he sold out. I think he only got about five million dollars for the yard.

In 1961, contracts came up for negotiation at the yard in Saint John and also at the yards in Halifax and Dartmouth. I sat in on the negotiations and for the first time there appeared to be collusion between the managements in Saint John and in Halifax.

As a rule, the yards had been competitive with each other. They never knew too much about what the other had offered. But in 1961, it appeared that Dosco and Irving were acting together. Their *modus operandi* was one meeting and one offer, x number of cents. Their demands were almost identical. A three-year contract, no flexibility, no negotiations. The first offer was the last offer. It became apparent to us in the membership that we had to strike to show that they couldn't sabotage or throw the collective bargaining process out the window.

We were perhaps a bit ambitious, taking on Irving and Dosco at the same time, especially since we weren't in the best graces with Congress and some of the labour movement. The steelworkers and a number of other unions were actually hoping we would get slaughtered so they could pick up our members. Unfortunately, the labour movement isn't always as solidified as it should be.

So we went through the process of strike vote. Management didn't call us in. They were calling our bluff. In the end, there was no bargaining room. We had to go on strike. Halifax went out first. It was just a matter of days, and Saint John went out.

There were actually four locals involved. Local 13 at Dartmouth Marine in Dartmouth and Local 1 at the Halifax Shipyards. Both were owned by Dosco. Then there was Local 3 at the Saint John Dry Dock and Local 6 at Saint John Ironworks. Both of these were owned by Irving.

After we went out, the company started hiring scabs right away to keep the yards going. In Saint John, within the week, they had put in trailers and a cafeteria so people could live right there.

Irving got an injunction against a bunch of us that we were not supposed to go at or near the plant. I went anyway and went on the picket line. In the meantime, Irving had put an ad in the paper that he was looking for men, announcing the wage rates and all that. John Parks—the plant manager at the time—came running out of the building and he said, "We've got you this time, Bell. You're breaking the injunction. I'm calling the RCMP and you'll be charged with contempt."

And I said, "Well, I don't think you can charge me with contempt." And he said, "Why not?"

"Well," I said, "I'm seriously considering your offer. You made an offer in the paper that people who were interested in coming to work at the dry dock should come out," I said. "If the terms are good enough, I'm going to go in there to work." And he used a bit of profanity and walked away.

Archie Kerr was also a manager in Saint John. Parks was his boss. So Kerr was sent up to Quebec to try to get some scabs to come down and work in the yard. The unions up there escorted him right back down to the train and sent him out. They said, "Don't you come up here again." We had a mutual aid agreement with the Quebec shipyard workers. Kerr thought he could go up and find guys to scab on us but he was wrong. He told us later, he was frank about it, he said, "I was afraid for my life. Those fellows told me to get on that goddamn train."

The manager at the Halifax shipyards was a Mr. Lezie. He was a fair man. There was a navy vessel in the yard for repair and normally the ship's crew would live aboard. Some of our more militant guys wanted to keep the navy guys from going down to their ship. With the strike, you never knew if a guy was going in to work or what. So we devised a pass system. People could go in the yard as long as they weren't going to take our jobs and we'd give them a pass. We even gave Lezie a pass just as a joke. Because of that, he thought we were kind of responsible. We held the brakes on the guys who were saying, "Let's get these guys, let's blow 'er up."

There wasn't any production in Saint John during the strike although the company always said there was. We had one guy killed in there just after the strike started, a scab. He was electrocuted. He hit the boom. After that, they stopped work. In

Halifax, the company made the foremen go into the shops and turn the equipment on to make noises, that kind of thing. They'd operate the odd crane but they weren't really doing production.

We had a public meeting at a high school auditorium in Saint John and wives of the strikers were there to tell people about the strike. The wives didn't go on the picket line, not then. But they would volunteer in other ways. Some of them would get on a telephone campaign, get after the politicians, or they'd go through their own political party circles.

One of the leaders who emerged during this time was Joe McLeod in Saint John. Joe was just a young fellow, a rank and filer. He was just starting to get involved in the union. Joe reminded me a bit of Milfred Hubley. Milfred would never ask you to explain something. He'd make a ridiculous statement about something, and invite an argument from you in order to get information. That was his style, and it was Joe's too. Both were kind of too shy or too reserved to admit when they didn't know something. Joe would do that even with management. Lots of times, he would know that things he was putting forward were inaccurate, but he'd do it to get information out of the company.

From the 1961 strike on, Joe was a leader in Saint John. He was either president of the local or vice-president. Even when he wasn't on the executive, he would stay on the negotiating committee so that often the company saw Joe as having more influence than the president of the local. In the early 1970s, for example, there was a walk-out in Saint John over health and safety conditions. The "nine-day war," they called it. Government finally brought in a mediator, Doug Stanley, who did a big report. Victor Rabinovitch came down from the CLC in Ottawa. He was involved in health and safety issues. So indirectly Joe was one of the people who were responsible for getting changes to the occupational health and safety act in New Brunswick, that you had the right to refuse to work in unsafe conditions.

In 1961, it was the first time that we had joint negotiations at the yards in Saint John with the craft unions. Irving MacAskill, a machinist, was chairman of the negotiations. We actually loaned money to one of the craft unions—the IBEW—to pay their members strike benefits because the electricians' union had no benefits. There was about 20 or so of them in the electrical department. In order to have them out with us, so that they wouldn't cross the picket line, we had to loan them money. Here we were, a small Maritime union, and we were loaning money to an international. I don't think we ever got that money back.

We had a conciliation officer in a few times and then we got a breakthrough. I think there was a difference of four cents over a three-year agreement but the companies also dropped a number of their other demands, things we already had that they wanted reduced. For example, they wanted you to work 40 hours before you went on overtime. The way it worked, if I missed a day of work due to sickness, then got called in on Saturday, I still got my time and a half for Saturday. What they wanted was to say, if you were off Tuesday or Wednesday, you'd be on straight time when you came in on Saturday. But they dropped that demand.

We could see the membership was getting worried—no work, and the union was running out of funds. A motion was made that it be left to the discretion of the executive committee to settle the strike if they thought it was an honourable settlement. The executive had the power to sign. In retrospect, we probably should have held mass meetings with the membership because as a result the yard in Saint John was left uneasy. There was some bitterness among the men. We were caught under pressure, wanting to get the contract settled. We gave away three hours of double time for time and a half. That's what the companies insisted they needed in order to get them to sign the contracts. The union was able to regain that in subsequent negotiations.

In every strike, there's always a bitterness. I felt that for two corporations that had wanted to dictate to the workers what their conditions should be—and that had been in collusion— that we had at least broken up that strategy. Dosco wouldn't dare do that with the miners or steelworkers but they were going to do it with us, the shipyard workers. I thought that because of the strike, we stood a chance in the future. Otherwise, we would have been on the defensive from then on.

It was the biggest and the longest strike the Marine Workers' Federation had ever pulled off. It lasted 11 weeks. A lot of the unions thought we were a little bit irresponsible in taking on two of the biggest corporations in eastern Canada at one time, especially since we weren't part of a big union with a lot of resources.

Many unions in those days operated from hand to mouth but we were fortunate in having good secretary-treasurers of our locals and our locals were frugal. We had a lot of bonds and savings. I think the rest of the labour movement was a bit astounded at what we had. We had made friends with so many different unions—Angus and I assisting other unions; guys like Joe McLeod would go on any kind of a picket line; any kind of dispute in the city and they would call the Marine Workers to send over some pickets. As a result, our relations with a lot of unions in the Atlantic region and across Canada were very good. No matter what appeal would come in, we would always send something.

So during the 1961 strike, we sent Gordon Smith to central Canada on a fundraising mission. Gordon Smith was the business agent for Local 1. He was a very, very emotional person. If you told him a sad story, he'd cry. I remember one time we were at a CLC convention and they had Cesar Chevarez from the grape workers union in the United States. He gave a speech and showed pictures of how farm workers, women and children, were treated in California. Gordon threw his whole wallet into the collection box. There was a woman sitting next to him who took it out and took a ten or whatever and threw it back in but gave him back his wallet. He was crying his eyes out.

So Gordon went to Ontario to talk to mine and smelter workers up north and steel workers in Hamilton, to tell them about our strike and to ask for assistance.

We thought taking on Dosco and Irving at the same time was just something that we couldn't sidestep or avoid. It was very difficult because of the fact that Irving was known as quite a union buster around the province. I knew the way Irving operated. I had been on a conciliation board for the veneer workers in Saint John back in the 1940s. They never worked Sundays, even though it was war time. They always worked overtime at night and on Saturdays, but never on Sundays.

But in the contract, it said double time for Sundays. Irving seized on that excuse in negotiations. "I'm not paying double time," he said. It was probably one of his only collective agreements that said double time on Sundays and he'd be damned if the veneer workers were going to set a pattern for him. One of his big demands was that the clause be taken out of the agreement. The union refused and the workers were forced out on strike.

So they set up a conciliation board. McGowan was Irving's nominee. I was the union nominee and we sat down. K.C. Irving was there and he said, "I'll be damned if I'm paying anyone double time. No workman is worth double time." So I asked him how many Sundays the men had worked. I said, "Would it be true that since this contract was signed, no Sundays have been worked?"

Well, he blew his cork. We had to stop the hearing. "I'm not listening to any communist at this hearing," he said. This was common language, a lot of blunt language at that time. "I'm not letting any damn communist come in here and challenge my word."

So the chairman said, "Now, now, we'll adjourn the meeting. This is getting out of hand." So we went into the back room and I was just waiting for the old judge to start balling me out. I figured he was an Irving man. As soon as we got in the back room, he started laughing. He said, "That's the first time I've ever seen anyone rile up K.C. Irving as much as you did. You really got under his skin." And here I was just ready to jump on him for being an Irving man, to give him a blast. I was kind of short fused in those days.

After that, Irving moved the veneer plant out of Saint John. Actually, it was the "bronze beetle" infecting the wood that convinced him to move the plant to Ontario, but that strike was never settled. He just moved the plant out and turned the building into a garage for buses. There had been about 80 guys at the plant. It was Angus MacLeod who had organized that plant. It was their second contract that they went out on strike for.

Another time, we lost a local in Liverpool because of the fact that it was an Irving yard. The company offered a settlement with a wage increase but no union security. The workers asked me what my view was and I said, "Well, I think that if you go back in after you have been out now for 49 days, if you go back in without union security, it's not going to be too long before there'll be no union." And that's what took place. They had assured me, "Oh yes, we'll keep the union together." But bit by

"Back in the fold." Jim Bell was re-elected to the N.S. Federation of Labour executive in 1965 as secretary-treasurer. With him are president John Lynk (right) and vice-president Clarie Webber (middle).

bit, the company got rid of the militants and hired other guys and the first thing you knew, the union was gone.

* * *

Anti-communism started to ease up towards the mid-1960s. By 1965, when I was elected secretary-treasurer of the Nova Scotia Federation of Labour, it had pretty well beat itself out. There had been a lot of ridiculous stuff, you know, that John Steinbeck's book *Grapes of Wrath* was communistic, that Steinbeck himself was a communist. People at different libraries would have debates as to whether or not to carry his books or whether they should be banned. It got so that they even started to debate whether or not they should carry a lot of the established literature of the day. Someone was always finding hidden communist messages, whether it was poetry or literature. After a while, it got to the point where people were saying, "This is lunacy."

After the merger [of the two N.S. Federations of Labour] in 1956, Hugh MacLeod had been elected secretary-treasurer. He was a friend of mine and we used to discuss certain legislative objectives that we thought we should be pursuing. Then after Hugh, Sinclair Allen took over as secretary-treasurer. Hugh, Sinclair and I always used to get together, discuss these things, have a little drink. The right wing in the federation didn't like that and used to get after them to stop fraternizing with me. They'd make caustic remarks, "Don't be influenced by him. He's going to brainwash you." Somehow I had psychic powers. I was going to put them under my control.

I never really went out of my way to deny or explain my views. I'd get into an argument with people about different things that were going on in the world. But I never made any public announcements or that sort of thing. Someone would say, "Why don't you make a public declaration of your position?" But I wouldn't. I wasn't plotting to overthrow the regime or anything like that. Through the educational process, I was telling people that they could organize and in some kind of organized, systematic way, they could improve their standards—through the trade union movement, a social democratic party, the communist party or whatever vehicle they wanted to use. I didn't go around saying, "There's only one choice. This is how you should vote. This is what you should strive for." I said, "Choose your own vehicle."

So Sinclair Allen was secretary-treasurer of the federation and he became a CLC representative. The policy of Congress was that once you went on Congress staff, you were supposed to get out of any position on the federation executive because that took up too much of your time. So Sinclair wanted to resign but Congress asked him to stay on another year. They wanted to prepare someone to take over as secretary-treasurer. They were afraid it would be me, that I would move in to fill the void, so to speak. I think Congress recognized that as I was on good terms with him and the delegates, once Sinclair left that I would get it.

I was nominated at the 1965 convention at the Isle Royale Hotel in Sydney. I remember that I made a speech to the convention and I put a little bit of dramatics into it. I paraphrased a statement that John L. Lewis had made at one time, that the labour movement would sooner elect a guy who was a whiskey-drinking, cigar-smoking, poker-playing son-of-a-gun than a pure rank-and-filer who wanted to represent the workers. By that time, most of the delegates knew me and they got a big kick out of that. So they elected me.

I was pleasantly surprised that I was elected. By that time, we had assisted a lot of unions in their difficulties. For example, we had helped the seafood workers—first led by Roy Keefe and later by Lawrence Wilneff—in their negotiations and arbitration or conciliation. We'd been on a lot of picket lines. When other unions were on strike, a marine worker was always there.

CHAPTER TEN
The Co-op Movement

During the 1961 strike, the money started to run out. We had four locals out at the same time and we had to raise about $25,000 a week in the Halifax area and a lesser amount in Saint John. A lot of our money was tied up in bonds. I had gone to the manager at the Royal Bank on Gottingen Street before the strike started and I said to him, "We might be heading into a labour dispute this year. If we do, can we borrow against our bonds, use them as collateral?"

And he said, "How much would it be?"

"Probably about $300,000 or so," I said.

And he said, "I don't see any reason why not."

I had my own account there. I knew this guy and he was a pretty good fellow.

So a couple of days before the strike started, I went to see him again and I said, "Well, we're ready to turn over the bonds and borrow against them." And he said, "God, I can't do it, Bell. Our solicitor says it can't be done because you're an unincorporated body. The only way we could recover our money would be to go to every member and get them to sign off their interest in the bonds." He mentioned the solicitor's name and it was the same solicitor that Dosco had. So that kind of made me mad. And I said, "What the hell. We'll sell." So we called up a stockbroker and sold the bonds. We took a loss on them because the market was down at the time. And we said to ourselves, "After this strike is over, we'll fix that up."

So after the strike, I went to the labour council and I said, "We should start a credit union for the trade union movement." So we did and we called it the Capital Credit Union. I knew this young fellow, Eric Dean, who was going to Dalhousie University at the time in commerce. So I said, "I think we can talk him into running our credit union. We can't run it full-time and he can't do it full-time because he's in school but he can do it evenings and Saturdays." Our members were only available evenings and Saturdays anyway because they were mostly working the day shift.

So Eric became manager of the Capital Credit Union. We got an office in the carpenters' hall. Alice had a beauty parlour just down the hall and anyone who came in, she agreed to take their deposits and give them a receipt. Eventually, it got so big that we had to hire a guy full-time. We hired a fellow by the name of Bob Watters and we went full-time and moved up the street into a storefront on Gottingen.

After a while, we merged with St. Pat's and a credit union in Spryfield. They were very small credit unions so we picked up their assets and their members. The plumbers had their own credit union and they came in with us, too. We called it the Halifax Metro Credit Union. This was around 1970. I had been president of Capital and I became president of Metro. Between the two of them, I was president for 20 years.

At the time in the co-op movement, there wasn't too good a feeling about workers unionizing. We were in the League Savings and Mortgage Company, an umbrella group of all the credit unions. But we made it clear to the League that we would go back to the banks if in any way they denied the workers the right to join a union. So the workers eventually got unionized in a CLC directly-chartered local. A fellow by the name of Hanratty represented them and signed their first contract.

In the meantime, Eric graduated and went to work for B.A. Oil. He didn't like it much and I kept nagging at him, "What the hell are you working for the private corporations for. Why don't you work for the public sector, the ordinary people, a co-op or credit union or something like that?" So that's when we started a store. Eric and his wife Eleanor [Alice's daughter] became quite active in starting the co-op store in Dartmouth, along with people like Reg Bell, Winston Settle and Perry Ronayne. It was the second co-op store in Canada that was direct charge. The first one was in Ottawa. We had about 700 members.

After that, we organized a direct charge co-op in Saint John. I remember going up there with Eric. Bob Lockhart was a radio commentator. He said he wouldn't join a co-op himself but he gave us a whole morning on his radio program to talk about co-ops, and we got people who were interested to phone in. So we got a nucleus of people who were interested and they started a direct charge co-op on the Golden Mile. The Marine Workers' Federation lent them money to rent a warehouse and turn it into a store. Since then, three other co-op stores have started in Saint John.

Eric had made contact with Co-op Atlantic—it was called Maritime Co-operative Services at the time—and they offered him a job so he quit B.A. Oil and went to work for Co-op Atlantic. He was the representative in Nova Scotia. After a while they asked him to move to Moncton and he took up another position. He eventually became assistant manager and today he's general manager of Co-op Atlantic.

The Marine Workers' was one of the early unions in the Maritimes that bought saving certificates from Maritime Co-op Services. I was interested in the co-op movement because my philosophy was that all these movements were necessary, that no one movement was the answer.

* * *

We also got into co-op housing. Housing was at a premium in Halifax so some of the fellows in the shipyards came and wanted to start a co-op. We called it the Sackville Housing Group. We were unsuccessful getting land out in Sackville so we started looking at some vacant land in behind of Bayers Road on St. Andrew's Avenue. There were 45 lots. We contacted three other co-op groups—co-op groups were organized in a dozen or so families—and we put together about 45 families in four co-op groups. The other three groups asked me to be their spokesman before City Council to get the land.

We went down to City Hall. Richard Donahoe was Mayor of Halifax at the time. This was in the 1960s. Abby Lane was the only woman on council. We put in a bid of $22,500 and went to speak before the committee of the whole. They turned us down. So we went to a council meeting that night. It was the same members. In the committee of the whole, it had been five for the proposal and six against. At city council, we managed to get it reversed, six for, five against, but we had to raise our bid to $45,000 for 45 lots.

I made a speech to the effect that this was a group of working people who were trying to get housing for themselves, that they should be commended and assisted. They were going to borrow $6,500 each from the Nova Scotia Housing Commission, and Alderwoman Lane got up and said, "I don't know much about co-ops but I'm a little bit leery of it. It kind of smells like the type of thing that they do in Russia."

So I said to the mayor, "You know, Mr. Donahoe, I hardly think so, because of the fact that if that's the case, then St. F.X. University and Monseigneur Coady are undercover agents for the Comintern." And Donahoe said, "Enough of that, Bell." But then he said to Mrs. Lane, "You're absolutely wrong. The co-op movement is a legitimate movement and the government of Nova Scotia is supporting it through the Housing Commission." So we got the lots on St. Andrew's Avenue and we started co-op housing.

* * *

The next thing we did was start a burial society. There were two or three members in the Universalist Church, myself and a few others. We had heard about this idea from the United States. We started at a church down on Inglis Street. A fellow by the name of Vickery was the pastor at the time. People paid $5 to join. We negotiated a list for services with certain undertakers— not all of them would co-operate—so we used to recommend that people go to either J. Albert Walker or Mattatalls.

Funerals were $450 or even less if you didn't want certain services, if you wanted a simple pine box and closed casket. A lot of the clergy supported us in this. It is called the Greater Halifax Memorial Society, and still operates but there's no office, just a phone number.

After that, we started a co-operative oil company. We had an oil truck that went around delivering oil. That failed because we were too spread out. People out in Bedford would want $10 worth of oil and the next delivery would be on St. Margaret's Bay Road. So the cost of transporting small amounts of oil was too much.

> *"J.K. would give you the shirt off his back. I remember one time Jim lost his wallet—$300, all gone. So a couple days later we were in the club and a little kid came in with the wallet, but it was empty. And Jim said, 'Where's my money?' And the kid said, 'My mother took it.' And I said, 'Holy geez, Jim, call the police.' But he said, 'No, ole boy, we'll let it go. She probably needed it more than me.'"*
>
> —Leo McKay, executive director
> **Nova Soctia Federation of Labour**

I was also a volunteer for burying paupers, fellows who would pass away who didn't have family or anyone in Halifax. There were a few names that you'd call to get people together to act as pallbearers. I remember one time I was supposed to get a group together and I got so busy with negotiations that I forgot. The undertaker called me up and he said, "Bell, you know, I've got a body here that we've got to bury." So I said, "Let's make it Saturday. I guarantee I'll be there Saturday."

So Saturday morning, I went down to the Marine Workers' Club and said to Bomber, the bartender, "Give the boys a drink." After he did, I said, "Now I gave you a drink for a purpose, boys. I need a fellow buried, a pauper. I need some pallbearers. And I can't seem to round up enough fellows. So how about it. Let's go out and bury him." So we went out and did it. The fellow was about three or four days overdue.

In another case, there was a woman died and her two daughters were there and they got fighting among themselves for her ring. And one says, "Mommy said I could have the ring." And the other says, "You're a goddamn liar, she said I could have it." They got into a real fight there at the graveyard. The funeral director—he was kind of a diplomatic guy—he put his arms around them and said, "Don't you think it would be better if you let your mother keep the ring and take it to heaven with her?" And he gave me a big wink. But when I saw those grave diggers there, I said to myself, "She won't be taking the ring to heaven with her. After the pall bearers and the funeral procession have left, that ring will be going to the nearest pawn shop."

One time, this fellow came into the club. He asked for me and I identified myself and he said, "I'm the brother of the fellow that you apparently helped to bury some time ago. I just wanted to thank you." He said his brother had come to Halifax from Ontario but he had never gotten in touch with the family. They didn't know where he was. So we just shook hands and he thanked me. There were a lot of transients in Halifax. Sometimes, they didn't want their families to know where they were.

* * *

There are people who belittle the labour movement and others who belittle the co-op movement. I don't think that's right because we all make a contribution towards the betterment of working people. What's needed is more unity, among the trade union movement and among the co-op movement, to protect the rights and standards of ordinary people. Some people get carried away. "I belong to the trade union movement and the labour movement is the whole answer." Well, I don't believe that. I don't believe the co-op movement is the whole answer. But all of us working together can be a force for social betterment.

CHAPTER ELEVEN

Fighting for Legislative Changes

Once I was re-elected to the executive of the Nova Scotia Federation of Labour in 1965, I purposely confined myself to pushing for legislative improvements. I stayed away from what I considered a frivolous type of approach. I studied acts that existed in other provinces and made recommendations that similar acts be passed here. We would always show that what we were asking for was already in effect somewhere else. We weren't asking to break new ground. We still had a lot of catching up to do in the Atlantic provinces, in legislation and in collective agreements. We were just trying to bring workers in Nova Scotia up to the standards that existed elsewhere. In this effort, Leo McKay, the executive secretary of the federation, did and still does provide valuable research help.

I used to get up at conventions and speak on different issues. Not only at conventions but also when the executive went before the government. If there were certain things that I felt that they had missed in their brief for legislative change, I'd wait until they finished, then I'd get up and speak.

For example, I think I played a little part in getting changes made to the pension act over the years. I was also part of the group that went after the government to get the denturists legalized. The government finally struck a compromise that denturists could do full dentures but not partials. The result was that working people could get dentures made for less money.

One time I appeared before Fraser Mooney of the Liberals. He was chairman of the Law Amendments Committee. We wanted to speak on safety. So he said, "We have a lot of cases here, Bell.

Perhaps rather than read your brief you could make a brief summary." So after about an hour of talking—I could have read the brief in 15 minutes—Mooney said, "There's one thing I've learned, never to ask you to summarize."

I also used to come up with ideas to create jobs. When Gerry Regan was Minister of Trade, we used to have little sessions on the economy and I used to suggest different things. You know, why can't the Americans buy more of our apples, more of our potatoes.

I met the deputy premier of China in Halifax once. We were at a convention of the Nova Scotia Federation of Labour and Gerry Regan brought him down. He wanted me to meet him. It so happened that I had a couple books by the leader of China, the sayings of Mao Tse-tung, so I got him to autograph them. I gave one to Johnny Lynk, who was president of the federation at the time, and the other to one of the secretaries, Glenda Cooper. She said she'd prize it.

So I got talking to the deputy premier about resources. He was also the minister of energy in the Chinese government. We got talking about possible trade with China and I told him, "Incidentally, on account of your country, I almost got thrown out of the labour movement." He said, "How's that?" So I told him about the incident in Ottawa where I was on the mike hollering for recognition of China and A.R. Mosher cut me off. We both got a big chuckle out of that. We had a drink of whiskey together.

Another time, there was a representative from the Soviet Academy of Sciences who came to Halifax and he wanted to talk to a trade unionist. Harry Flemming was Gerry Regan's assistant at the time, and Flemming and Regan steered the guy to me. So we shook hands, sat down and started talking. And first thing I said, "Jesus, you fellows over there in the Soviet Union are making it awful hard for us left-wingers over here to justify some of your actions." And he said, "Why?"

"Well," I said, "there's a guy by the name of Keenan. He runs a Pepsi Cola company in the US, and he was one of the guys who financed Pinochet to overthrow Allende in Chile. Now, you made a deal with him to take his equipment and bottle Pepsi over there in the Soviet Union. Christ almighty, you picked out a capitalist in the US who was in on the scheme to kill the democratically-elected head of Chile." And he said that he wasn't aware of that and he scribbled down some notes. I said, "I don't go along with that, that you're doing business with a guy who's a supporter of Pinochet."

One time, I went before Tom McInnis, the minister of industry, and I said, "A bunch of our guys in the shipyard are laid off. They live down the eastern shore. Before they came to work in the shipyard they were fishermen. Why don't you help them get together and get a mussel growing plant started, you know, growing mussels for restaurants, that kind of thing."

He said, "Well, that seems to be a good idea. Are you looking for a piece of the action?"

"No, I'm not. I'm just making a suggestion," I said. "I don't want any shares or anything."

So they set it up. We got the department of fisheries to put some money in and encourage fishermen down there to grow cultivated mussels. There's four or five outfits down there now.

Another time, I went before David Nantes and I said, "You're promoting a causeway and generating plants across the Minas Basin. I've got some ideas about that too. I think you should develop it on the following basis. The world's biggest inland fish farm. Sole, flounder. Aquaculture, you know. Put a roadway over it—don't just put the generating station—so that truckers from the Annapolis Valley can save 100 miles going to central Canada with their produce. Establish it so that we have marinas and such for recreation. A body of water that will be protected, that won't be subject to the wind and storms as the open parts of the Bay of Fundy are. Make it a multi-purpose type of thing."

When they were talking about the pipeline coming down here from Quebec City, I went to Buchanan and I said, "For a few extra dollars make that line reversible so that when you strike gas off Sable Island you'll be able to ship it out." Of course, at that time, there was the big promise of gas on Sable Island.

At one point Walter Fitzgerald—he was labour minister—he said, "I'm going to give up my job, Bell, and take hold of one of those schemes that you're talking about."

I was also a director of Industrial Estates for a few years. We had suggested to Robert Stanfield that he set up the agency and so he gave the labour movement a chance to be represented on it. Sinclair Allen had been a director when he was secretary-treasurer of the federation and I replaced him.

I remember one time we wanted to meet with the Council of Maritime Premiers. They were meeting up in Newcastle and they said, "No, we don't meet with delegations." And we said, "We're coming up anyway. We want an appointment. We'll meet with you if we have to follow you around into restaurants or hotels or what have you." So they agreed and we met with them. We had a position on shipbuilding, a program that we wanted the government to introduce, and they endorsed it. They had no problem with it. But they told us afterwards, "Don't advertise this because the Council of Maritime Premiers is a private meeting. Once we get started meeting with delegations, we won't be able to do our own business." That was in the 1980s. We had two hours with them.

So we'd get to know all these legislators, all these politicians. They'd even let their hair down at different times and tell us what they could or couldn't do, what they're told not to do, that kind of thing. They'd share their frustrations with us.

* * *

Coming up with all these ideas, in a way it was a contradiction. But for me, the issue wasn't who took the profits. It was the question of getting the industry and putting people to work. I'm realistic enough to believe that Nova Scotia isn't going to determine the political future of Canada. It's an under-developed province in an under-developed region. I'm sure they have under-developed regions even in socialist countries that could profit by joint ventures with the private sector.

You take us poor provinces. We have a medical school in Dalhousie and the cost of tuition doesn't pay the cost of educating these people. I believe that it's not unfair for the state to say, "We've given you an education, you have to spend the next five years in a particular area, the poorer part of the country or the province."

I presented that idea once to Richard Donahoe when he was minister of health. And he said, "You can't do that Bell, that's totalitarianism." So I said, "Well then, you explain to me, Mr. Minister, why that applies to teachers and nurses. They're the sons and daughters of working people and after they come out of the teachers' college in Truro, you've got a rule that the province can hold them back and use their services. The same with nurses. But when it comes to doctors or engineers or scientists, they're free agents. They can go to Hollywood and take pimples off a movie actress's bum. It's a double standard."

We were graduating 30 dentists a year so why does a person in Canso have to travel all the way to Antigonish to get his tooth pulled when he has a toothache? I believe we have a right to say, "We gave you four or five years of education, we need three or four years from you." But Donahoe didn't agree.

Some people have the idea that the labour movement is always hollering to the boss, "Give me more, give me more, give me more." But the labour movement also attempts to obtain legislation and to push for job development, things like that the public isn't really aware of.

In our fight for legislative change, we always had good help from labour lawyers, especially those connected at the time with the Kitz-Matheson firm—Raymond Larkin, Gerry McConnell and Ron Pink—as well as others like Blaise MacDonald.

CHAPTER TWELVE
Union Organizing

There were very few strikes in the Atlantic provinces that the Marine Workers' Federation wasn't somehow involved in. One of the big ones was the fishermen's strike in Canso in 1970.

There were a number of herring seiners that had moved from British Columbia. Some of these fellows who worked on the boats had been union members out west. So they wrote back that conditions down east were naturally below the standards that they had enjoyed and that their union should do something about it, help them out in some way.

Homer Stevens, who worked for the fishermen's union in BC, came to Halifax and he met with John Lynk, myself, and Leo McKay. And he said, "We haven't got the resources and we may get a chance to get into the CLC but one of the conditions is that we stay in British Columbia. [The United Fishermen and Allied Workers' Union had been expelled in the 1950s by the TLC for communist leanings.] Congress doesn't want us to become a national union. But," he said, "the fellows are asking us to come in. We wouldn't come in if some other union here has better resources and has representatives within the area to organize them." Apparently no one else was interested—everyone knew it was going to be a tough fight—so we said to him, "Go ahead. Even though you're not affiliated to Congress, the Nova Scotia Federation of Labour is a Congress affiliate, so go ahead."

Homer Stevens is a good guy. Very intelligent, very methodical. He kept a kind of ongoing diary of events. He could write up a good report or make a good argument.

But what happened was that they got into a strike situation in Canso and then some of the fellows in the federation began to waffle as to whether or not Homer Stevens should be here because of the fact that he was a communist. Homer also made a basic mistake by taking a group of hippies with him to Canso. They weren't workers with any experience in the trade union movement but a bunch of young fellows and women who lived a hippie lifestyle, sort of an intellectual crowd from Halifax. Some of the established labour representatives sneered at Homer for doing that.

A lot of people began taking the position that perhaps the solution was for the United Fishermen and Allied Workers' Union (UFAWU) to get the hell back to British Columbia and that would solve the problem. I took the position that that wouldn't solve it. They had started organizing and what was needed was support to finish the job. The whole issue split the federation.

John Lynk was a bit uneasy about the fact that it looked as if Homer Stevens would be chased out of the province. Lynk was also a vice-president of Congress by virtue of the fact that he was president of the Nova Scotia Federation of Labour. But at the same time, every union was looking for membership, including his. Lynk was with Retail Wholesale.

What happened was that the CLC apparently suggested a committee be set up, with a representative from the federation along with the fishermen and St. Francis Xavier University. St. F.X. kind of took the initiative. Leo McKay was named from the federation and during the course of the thing they practically made a deal and wrote an agreement. It was an agreement between the company and no specific organization, just a committee of the workers. The settlement was that the employer agreed to give fishermen certain conditions provided that they didn't join the UFAWU. Leo thought it was the best solution at the time.

I didn't agree with St. F.X. taking the initiative and moving it out of the trade union movement's hands. And we didn't agree with the settlement. We said, "We can't support this because of the fact that it means that if an employer doesn't like a union,

One of Jim's longtime friends is former Nova Scotia premier Gerald Regan. Regan attended the Marine Workers' Federation convention in Moncton in 1979, and had his picture taken with the federation executive. Jim is shown far right, Regan, second from right.

he can just go through that process and the first thing, he'd be having a say in which union he was going to do business with."

It was actually a contravention of the trade union act that said a worker has the right to join the union of his choice. The decision to sign with the committee of workers became the way in which the company got rid of the BC union. After that, the CBRT&GW (Canadian Brotherhood of Railway and Transport & General Workers) was called in to organize the trawlermen.

The Canadian Food and Allied Workers' Union eventually went in there and signed a contract in Canso. We had a meeting at the Labour Temple and one of the fellows got up to explain how it wasn't really a raid, that it was a case of the workers all wanting them in there, that they were the union the workers wanted. So I got up and challenged the guy, saying that wasn't true. The Marine Workers could have had them too but we

Whenever the Nova Scotia Federation of Labour held a demonstration, Jim Bell was always in the forefront of activity. Here he is on the left of the banner. This "Work for Wages" march was held in downtown Halifax during the early 1980s.

wouldn't play the part of being a strike breaker. There was collusion at the time between the international union and the company to get bargaining rights diverted to another union.

* * *

Another big labour issue during the 1970s revolved around Michelin Tire. The first group that tried to organize Michelin's plant at Granton in Nova Scotia [the company had a second plant in Bridgewater] was the Operating Engineers. This was in the early 1970s. They, in fact, had been going around the province, going to fishplants but also to shipyards, telling workers to "Get the hell out of the union you're in and come with us." They were actually raiding.

When it came to Michelin Tire, they didn't have a majority of the fellows at Granton, although they apparently did have a majority of the guys working in the powerhouse. So they put in an application for certification for the powerhouse. A day or two before the application was to be heard, Gerry Regan came out with an order-in-council that said that where an industrial plant was in existence, the Labour Relations Board need not certify a union that was carving out a craft, that didn't want to organize the whole shop—as an industrial union would—but only wanted to organize a particular trade within the shop.

Now technically, in principle, we supported that idea. We were an industrial union and that gave us an advantage. It gave us some protection from raids. It would stop them from coming around the shipyards because the board wouldn't let them carve out a craft union. But because of the fact that this order-in-council was passed as a tactic to defeat a union, we criticized Regan for the timing of it. He put it through just to safeguard Michelin from having a union.

Then the Rubber Workers tried to organize the plant in 1977 and again in 1979, and that's when the Buchanan government brought in the "Michelin bill." What it said was that where a company had more than one plant in the province and where it could be proven that the plants were interdependent, the union had to have a majority of workers in all the plants before it could be certified. In Nova Scotia you only have 90 days for a signing-up campaign, so the bill made organizing those two Michelin plants virtually impossible.

I remember we ran into John Buchanan on the stairway of the Legislative Assembly building. We said, "For God's sakes, why didn't you at least lengthen the term of the cards. Let us have a longer signing-up period than what it is now. While we still object to the thing in principle, it would at least reduce the irritation a little." So Buchanan seemed to kind of take that to heart and he went into his office. He must have called the Michelin lawyer—his office was one street over, one block away—because pretty soon the lawyer came running over and he went into Buchanan's office. We were there in the gallery

In 1971, J.K Bell was honoured at a testimonial dinner in Halifax. Both Premier G.I. Smith and Opposition Leader Gerald Regan paid tribute. The Halifax Chronicle–Herald *published the following editorial:*

RESPONSIBLE AND RESPECTED RADICAL

James K. Bell is a responsible and respected radical.

He's a professional trade unionist who's feared, yet admired, by those who have occasion to confront him across the bargaining table. He's fiercely dedicated to the cause of the working man, yet sensible and sympathetic if he believes the other side has a genuine problem. He's a self-trained debater, and a good one, and a well-versed graduate of the school of hard knocks.

He has come a long way from the day in 1934 when, at the age of 14, he launched his career as a union negotiator, seeking a five-cent hourly wage boost for the quarry workers in Saint John. Now, as secretary of the Nova Scotia Federation of Labour, he occupies one of the most important and influential offices in the province.

Last week, Jimmie Bell received the accolades of friend and foe alike at a testimonial dinner in his honour in Halifax. It was a tribute hard-earned and well deserved.

when Buchanan came in and we could tell that he had failed. That the Michelin lawyer had said, "No, no extension." We can't prove it but we're pretty sure because Buchanan just shook his head and went into his seat.

We believe that we had a majority at the plant in Granton. But, of course, we never found out because those ballots were all thrown out.

So that's what led to Lawrence Wilneff and myself leaving our government-appointed committee positions. The federation had a special convention and everyone said, "We'll get off every damn government board to protest the Michelin bill." I had been on the board of Industrial Estates, so I immediately wrote a letter to the president and resigned. Lawrence got off the Fishermen's Loan Board. But we were practically the only two. All the rest kept their appointments. That was a disappointment to me.

* * *

I'll tell you a story about how we turned an illegal strike into a legal strike. We got to know Albert Vincent in Saint John. He was the representative in the Atlantic region for the bricklayers' union, just a young man at the time. Sometimes at the dry dock, the steam boilers had to be relined with clay brick. If we didn't have the skilled men to do it, we had an arrangement with Albert that he would send over some of his men and we would let them do the work. Even though they were a craft union, we didn't object. And then, if he needed a labourer or such, and some of our guys were on lay-off, they'd go over there. Some of the building trades kind of frowned on that, but Albert used to say, "Well, I find these Marine Workers a good, sensible union." He used to defend us in TLC circles.

When Albert ran for City Council and got defeated, he said, "I'm not sure my mother voted for me because of the fact she's afraid I'd get into trouble. My brother wouldn't vote for me because he's a bit jealous. And my brother-in-law wouldn't vote for me because he'd listen to my sister. But I voted in that ward, and when the ballots were opened and counted, I had a big goose egg, zero." And Albert was ready to call up the United Nations to get his vote back. So I tried to say, "Albert, take her cool now. Anybody rags you about it, just say, I wasn't defeated, I was just delayed." And I told him about Lincoln being defeated nine times before he went on to become one of the greatest presidents of the US.

So in the early 1970s, there was a strike of the building trades down in Sydney against a Newfoundland fellow who owns a helicopter business, Craig Dobbin. What he was doing was trying to say, I want a carpenter to do bricklaying and so on. Mixing up the trades. The workers didn't like it so they pulled a strike. But it was an illegal strike because of the fact that most of the workers were under contract. The only ones on the job not under contract were the bricklayers and they weren't certified. They were all Newfoundlanders who had been brought over.

Just prior to that, Nova Scotia had changed its trade union act to allow for speedy certification of the building trades in three days. So Albert went to see the minister of labour at the time, Tom McKeough. He was actually sympathetic with the workers down in Cape Breton. He didn't want to see them in trouble. So Albert says, "If I can get speedy certification, that'll turn it into a legal strike and it'll take the heat off you and off the building trades in Cape Breton." So he got the okay from McKeough.

I went down to Sydney with Albert and we had a mass meeting at the steelworkers' hall. The minister of labour spoke and I spoke and Albert spoke and we explained our plan. We couldn't reveal it in its entirety. We had talked to the executive of the building trades and they were very skeptical, but enough of them at least had the sense to say, "Well, try it."

Meanwhile, the bricklayers had all gone home, so Albert got permission to fly them back to Cape Breton, signed them up and applied for certification. The minister was right there and we typed up the application for certification and gave it to him. Two days later, they were certified and they had the right to bargain. Dobbin wouldn't negotiate so we had to apply for conciliation, but in the meantime we were able to put up a legal picket line. The rest of the trades respected the line so the job was tied up. And that's how we turned an illegal strike into a legal strike.

* * *

I used to do organizing with Lofty MacMillan, the CUPE representative for the Maritimes. I remember one time we were organizing civic workers in Truro. We had stopped at a garage on the way into town so we decided to use this garage as our headquarters. We'd go around town and when we saw a civic employee working outside we'd ask him to jump in the car and we'd take him down to the garage. We'd take him into the washroom, show him the application form and explain that we were forming a union, and then we'd sign him up. Well, we did that so frequently that the fellow who operated the garage finally gave us some rather hard looks. I'm sure that he started to think we were a couple of homosexuals who were seducing fellow citizens. We laughed about that afterwards.

One time, Lofty and I were negotiating for the civic workers in Halifax. So we decided we'd have to pull a strike. Leonard Kitz was mayor at the time and we decided that we were going to have a strike the next day. So it was about two or three in the morning and I was asked to do the honour of calling the mayor to tell him that his workers would walk off the job at 8 a.m. So I got him out of bed, and I said, "Your worship, we just want to be fair about this. I'm going to tell you that at a late meeting tonight we decided we're going to have a strike tomorrow morning at 8 o'clock." And he said, "Get lost, Bell," and he slammed the phone down.

I went over to Marystown, Newfoundland while they were constructing the yard during the 1960s. I met with the workers. They weren't even being paid minimum wage. I told them how to get it, the procedures, that sort of thing. How to make a formal complaint. They said that when the yard got going they would contact me. So when the yard was finally built, I went over again. Lundrigan was the firm that was constructing the yard for the Newfoundland government and they, in turn, leased it to a Quebec firm that operated it.

That was the first and only local of the Marine Workers' Federation outside the Maritimes. There is a yard in St. John's but the building trades had that. That yard was part of the CN operation and the craft unions were already in there by virtue of the fact that they represented workers in 1949 when Newfoundland joined Confederation. So the Marine Workers' never went in. We never indulged in raiding. We left it up to the workers if they wanted to swing over into an industrial union.

Another place we organized was in Lunenburg. The Eisenhauers were an old Nova Scotia family. They owned a plant in Lunenburg, a foundry and machine shop in Bridgewater, and a yacht plant in Mahone Bay. The one in Mahone Bay was eventually turned into a fibreglass products plant, making large fibreglass units for emission control in smoke stacks, that kind of thing.

We'd been trying to organize them for years. Every year or two, I'd drop in. A couple of times I was ordered off the property, but that didn't faze me and the next time I'd go by, I'd drop in again. I'd go down around noon hour and the fellows would be sitting outside, eating their lunch. I'd appear and they'd get to know me. I'd say, "You fellows ready for unionization yet?" And I'd give them copies of our contracts in Saint John and Halifax. So I kept doing that.

Eventually, we met at the fishermen's hall in Lunenburg and they all signed up. We got the one in Lunenburg first, then the one in Bridgewater and the one in Mahone Bay. One of the guys in Mahone Bay—a chargehand that had ordered me out of the plant at one point, he was ready to call the RCMP—he eventually had a grievance that the union had to deal with. And he apologized and said he didn't know what the union was. Somebody had told him the workers were joining the Communist Party.

In those days, when you were trying to organize, they would call the police. The police didn't know anything about the status of unions and they'd come down and order you out. They'd even order you out of town. "We don't want no unions in this town." But then the police eventually got unionized themselves, so it's different today.

Workers would start to organize and someone would get fired and they'd say to me, "What should we do?" Some labour leaders would say, "Oh, we'll just go to arbitration." But I'd say, "Lookit brothers, firing a man for joining a union is a violent act. It's an economically violent act. My suggestion is to take job action." And immediately, the workers would put down their tools to protect their fellow brother.

That was a revolutionary concept. Others in the labour movement thought you should just go through arbitration but that would take a year or two and by that time the guy either couldn't get his job back or was no longer interested. It cost the union, and if the local didn't have any money, they couldn't go to arbitration because you had to pay your own lawyer. You had to pay half of the arbitrator's expenses. I would say the solution was to forget about procedure of law and take job action. That made me an oddball. That made me a communist.

What's the good of all this procedure, all this justice if you can't afford it, if the only way you can get justice is beyond your means?

CHAPTER THIRTEEN
Shipbuilding, Then and Now

Canada was one of the leading shipbuilding nations during the 1940s but since then we've seen a steady decline in the industry in our country, to the point where shipbuilding is now facing possible extinction.

For example, three decades ago, 98 percent of construction in Canadian shipyards was commercial vessel construction. In 1986, approximately 96 percent of new vessel construction was financed by government. So we now have a situation where shipbuilding is almost totally dependent on government.

The reason for such a drastic decline is due mainly to the fact that we are competing in a world market where the playing field is anything but level. Most shipbuilding nations around the world have put policies in place to aid and protect their shipbuilding industries while Canadian governments have not followed suit.

After World War II, there was a general decline in shipping and shipbuilding with the sale and/or transfer of tonnage registry to "flags of convenience" in countries that had little or no safety standards and minimum wages. A number of countries raised this concern with the United Nations, and a UN committee was formed on Trade and Development. UNCTAD began to recommend standards and a way for countries to share sea transport of exports and imports.

A formula of 40-40-20 was proposed whereby countries would carry 40 percent of their exports and imports in flag ships they controlled, their trading partner would carry another 40 percent, and the remaining 20 percent would be carried by flag ships

Jim Bell in 1978.

102 Ole Boy

 ## MARITIME MARINE WORKERS' FEDERATION

PRESIDENT
HARRY A. TAYLOR
VICE-PRESIDENT
W. Craig
SECRETARY-TREASURER
J. K. BELL

60 Gerrish St.
HALIFAX, N. S.
Phone 3-6039

M. Lowe
HlScotland.

EXECUTIVE MEMBERS
MILFRED HUBLEY

Affiliated to the Canadian Congress of Labour.

Representing the Majority of Organized Marine and Shipbuilding Workers in the Maritimes.

October 26th, 1949

Editor,
Chronicle-Herald
Halifax, N.S.

Dear Sir:—

As a representative of a labour organization which has direct interest in the present Canadian shipping slump, I welcome the opportunity of expressing our viewpoint and opinions on the matter.

While agreeing with Hon. Mr. L. Chevrier, Minister of Transport, when he states that the problem is world-wide, we disagree with his stated policy of "waiting out" the crisis before any Government action is taken.

Actually, Canada can maintain a merchant fleet of more than twice the present fleet size. Only 40% of our oil imports were carried in Canadian tankers in 1947, and we have lost several large tankers since then, leaving the present percentage lower than the 1947 figure. It is estimated that we would need an additional 200,000 tons (tankers) to carry all our oil imports.

Then again, in 1947 when we had a merchant fleet of over 1,000,000 tons, we carried only 20% of our exports and 27.9% of our imports. If we had legislation similar to that enacted in the U.S.A., which insists on 50% of goods carried in American bottoms, we would have to more than double our present fleet.

The term "Canadian Merchant Marine" generally leaves the impression that our fleet is owned by Canadian interests, yet actually only 22.7% of our fleet is Canadian controlled and the balance is controlled by foreign interests to the following degree: Greek – 39.6%; British – 13.8%; United States –

of a third country, largely ships from countries with "flags of convenience."

A number of countries adopted the UN formula but not Canada. If it had, it would have given us a volume of assured tonnage to carry in an updated merchant fleet. Canada would have been able to afford a merchant marine.

The latest generation of container ships, with their updated cargo handling equipment, their fast turnaround in port, and much smaller crews make such ships operated by industrial countries competitive with the older, slower, and larger-crewed vessels from "flags of convenience" countries. Our government in Ottawa, with a transport department usually headed by "land-lubber" lawyers, could not or would not see the importance of

15.7%. These figures were based on the 159 vessel deep-sea fleet as of
January of this year and may differ on the basis of the 118 vessel fleet at
the time of this writing.

Since the bulk of our fleet consists of the war-time built cargo and tanker
ships, which were built by public funds and sold to Canadian listed shipping
firms at a fraction of their value on the stipulation they would be retained
under the Canadian flag, we can ask if there is not a plan afoot to sell these
vessels abroad at a substantial profit.

Since there has not been a single hull built to replace the war-time built
ships which have been sold abroad, we would suggest that the Government
refund the shipping companies their actual capital involved and use the
remainder of the funds to build a number of modern efficient vessels which
could compete with foreign fleets; these ships to be either operated by the
Government directly or chartered to private shipping firms.

Labour organizations in other major shipping countries have recommended
that obsolete vessels be scrapped rather than sold to competitive shipping
interests abroad. If this is not acceptable to our Government, then at least the
funds realized through ships sold abroad should be ear-marked for modern
competitive replacements.

It is both tragic and unbecoming to have the ship owners make it appear
that the wages and living standards paid Canadian seamen and shoreside
workers is the chief factor in tying up Canadian vessels. This is an example
where workers who risked their very lives to keep the war-time merchant
fleet sailing are now told that they have received too much for their services
and must take pay cuts and job lay-offs.

A complete review of the situation should be undertaken by an immediate
Government Inquiry, and our Government should be prepared to implement
the necessary legislation to promote the industry as proposed above, taking
into account the interests of the taxpayers, the shipping industry and the
trade of our country, over the general demand of a hand-out to profiteering
ship-owners, many of whom are living abroad and are not especially interested in the promotion of Canadian shipping.

Yours truly,
J.K. Bell,
Secretary-Treasurer

a Canadian merchant fleet as a domestic tool of trade and
development.

A new generation of container ships are on the horizon,
incorporating revolving wind masts to cut fuel costs, more
advanced propulsion systems and cargo handling. With reduced
crews, wages are no longer the big factor. During World War II,
the Park vessels of 10,000 tonnes carried 30 to 35 crew members
while today, a container vessel of 100,000 tonnes has a crew of
about a dozen.

* * *

On August 17, 1987, the Marine Workers organized a demonstration at Province House in Halifax. At the time, we had about

16 guys working in the Halifax yard. Normally, there were close to one thousand. The *Louis St. Laurent* was supposed to be coming into the yard for a $120 million refit and that would have been the saviour of the Halifax yard. But the job kept being delayed. The refit was supposed to include a new bow section and there was talk that the government wanted to have it done elsewhere and then floated down to Halifax. In the meantime, the whole job was being delayed. They were letting it go by one budget so it would come up in the next.

I had retired but the union kept me on for six months afterwards as a general representative to do any kind of job that needed to be done. So we organized a demonstration in August. We wanted to put pressure on the provincial government to do more to get the *St. Laurent* down here and we wanted to announce a general shipbuilding policy. The Tories had issued a position on the shipbuilding industry during the 1984 election campaign and we wanted to hold them to it.

We had a meeting with Stewart McInnes, minister of trade, and we came out of the meeting and both me and Les [Holloway—then Local 1 business agent] were doing interviews with the media. One of the reporters asked Les what the marine workers would do if the demonstration didn't show any results and he said, "If they don't come to us, maybe we'll have to go to them." So we were walking away, and I said to Les, "Ole boy, are you serious? A demonstration in Ottawa?"

That's how the idea of going to Ottawa got started. It was Les's idea and he organized it. He was determined and he raised most of the money, going around to the different unions and speaking to meetings. It was supposed to be in October although it had to be delayed to give us time to raise more money. We finally got three buses—150 guys from Local 1 who went from Halifax to Ottawa, 22 hours on the bus. The executive flew up beforehand because of meetings with the Atlantic Tory caucus. Leo Walsh was president of the Marine Workers' at the time, Ricky Clarke was secretary-treasurer.

It was historic! A hundred and fifty guys coming all the way from Halifax to shake the government up. Afterwards, the boys went to different taverns, and the guys in the tavern said, "Are you the guys from Halifax." They'd seen them all on television, wear-

In late 1985, when Jim announced he was stepping down as secretary-treasurer of the Nova Scotia Federation of Labour, the Nova Scotia Worker published the following editorial, written by editor Michael Belliveau:

JK BELL STEPS DOWN

You see books on Roy Joudrey, the Nova Scotia financial and industrial multi-millionaire, or Frank Sobey, the commercial giant, but nothing on J.K. Bell whose life on the 'other side of the tracks' is truly a story of courageous commitment to the Canadian working people. At the thirtieth annual convention of the Federation of Labour, J.K. announced that he would not re-offer for the office of Secretary-Treasurer, a position he has held since 1965. Jimmy, as his colleagues refer to him, should now get down to the task of producing a book. He knows too much and has done too much not to have it recorded.

His schooling stopped at grade five; yet, he reads Dante's *Inferno* on Sunday afternoon, the *Wall Street Journal* over tea, the Bible in between Soviet journals and Latin American reports. He will expound on the rich heritage and Vatican influence of the little known Gregorian order of priests and then point out the technical problems at the Halifax shipyards. The unschooled Jim Bell will produce a written summary of the problems SYSCO has with tariffs and world markets, and he will put in verse the woes of the working man or the glories of a friend. And after he has given you the family tree of the Mayor of Halifax, he might tell you of the history of repression in Chile.

In his own Labour movement, J.K. Bell was hounded out as a 'communist' during the witch hunt McCarthy era that spilled over into Canada. In the Dirty Thirties, he organized in forced labour camps for the unemployed. He was harassed by the Toronto police and imprisoned by the federal authorities. Yet, premiers and prime ministers have sought him out for advice and Judges have deferred to his superior logic.

In some ways, it is no big deal that J.K. has stepped aside as the Federation's Secretary-Treasurer because it is hard to imagine that he will be any less influential as the guiding intelligence of the province's labour movement. J.K. worries about trendiness and careerism in the Labour movement and he worries about a resurgence of fascism in the Western World. His voice and his witness is not about to be muted because of a change in office. He remains in the Federation building as Secretary to the Marine Workers' Federation and you can bet his generous knowledge and insight will continue to be sought. In the meantime, let's have that book that will do credit to one of the Canadian working people's truly renewable resources!

ing their distinctive caps, so they bought them rounds of beer.

As a result of this demonstration, we were successful in advancing the start of work on the ice-breaker, converting her from steam to diesel, installing a new bow section, and removing all previously-installed asbestos insulation. This provided work for over 600 workers for over a year, and enabled the yard to tender on other work, providing jobs for more than 900 workers.

Les later led a group of workers who occupied the offices of the premier of Nova Scotia, Don Cameron, for not ensuring that offshore refit and repairs which involved provincial funding were not confined to Nova Scotian yards and workers. The premier finally agreed that some of this work should go to yards in the province, but while Les and the group were chastized by the media, no criticism was levied at the politicians.

* * *

One of the major issues facing us today is that the Canadian Arctic is still open to vessels of countries who fly "flags of convenience." It will take a major mishap before Canadians demand protection to our environment from unsafe shipping. If the Canadian Arctic was restricted to Canadian flag ships, we could ensure that higher standards of safety and inspection aboard vessel would take place.

Our politicians are currently reviewing constitutional changes for a better Canada. But they have so little faith in our country and its people, I cannot imagine that they would take the lead in an industry such as shipping and shipbuilding where we could lead the world.

CHAPTER FOURTEEN
Reflections

In the early days of trade unionism, the role that the labour movement played was basic and understandable to its membership. The role of the union was to introduce industrial democracy into the workplace. The fight for organization and for a collective agreement were cornerstone objectives. Improved wages and working conditions became by-products of these objectives. However, with experience, working people soon realized that many issues could not be settled at the bargaining table and had to be corrected or improved by political action. Legislative action was needed to provide a social safety net at times of sickness, lay-offs or injury on the job.

As new issues arose—safety in the workplace, international trade agreements, runaway enterprises—many enlightened trade unionists began preaching new roles for the trade union movement, encouraging alliances with community groups and political organizations to take united action against government or industry.

It was in this new role that I and others experienced the wrath of government agencies and employer groups—and even some parts of the labour movement— who wished us to confine our role to the collective bargaining table. There, they could take away our hard-fought gains by acts of collusion, inflation or legislative changes, while at the same time pointing the finger of blame at the so-called radical labour leaders.

When the two labour councils in Canada merged in 1956, they agreed that the bargaining rights and the jurisdiction of the various unions that existed would continue. It's written right in the constitution. Years ago, if I found a group of bakery workers who wanted to get unionized, I would contact the appropriate union or the CLC. Today that's not the case. Every union will take any group of workers that wants to get organized—provided there's enough in the group, that is. If it's five or six workers, to hell with them. But if there are a couple of hundred, if it's viable financially, take 'em in! Everybody's caught up in it because everybody's doing it.

At one time, the trend in industry was towards one central company, one big plant up in Toronto or within a 100-mile radius. Sixty-five percent of industry in the country was located in central Canada. But today, industry is getting smarter. Now the trend is towards decentralization so that if you have a strike, there's at least one plant that's either unorganized or organized into a different jurisdiction. One's with steel, the other's with the autoworkers, with a different contract renewal date. You can bet your boots that one plant will keep operating.

Because of these new strategies, the labour movement has to also develop new strategies. We have to develop a greater degree of responsibility and militancy, on the part of the leadership and the members. The old habit of taking strike action to solve every little problem has to be weighed against the possibility of success. Not that I'm against strike action. Strikes are still a needed and useful tool in the whole strategy of collective bargaining. You have to get your contract signed. But what I do say is that because of these new elements, we have to learn when to strike, how to strike, but also to be patient. We have to know when we're the anvil and bear it, to know when we're the hammer and strike.

That's one of the things that hasn't reflected itself yet in the labour movement. Not all the decline in union membership in the US, for example, has been because of plant closures. Our batting average of losing strikes has been a contributing factor. In a number of cases, workers have simply decided that they didn't want to belong to unions.

In a sense, history is repeating itself, the fact that in 1991, the federal government wouldn't go through collective bargaining with its civil service, that it wanted to impose zero, three and three percent wage increases and that's it, take it or leave it.

J.K. Bell at the Hotel Shediac in New Brunswick in 1991 with longtime friends Hugh MacLeod (left) and Sinclair Allen (right).

These are things that we experienced fifty years ago, having to fight for collective bargaining. After all our work, I wonder if the labour movement has advanced, has made gains.

* * *

As a socialist, I am naturally distressed over events pertaining to natural or human-made disasters. The splitting of the atom and the harnessing of nuclear energy were heralded as our entry into the technological age, and would provide a glut of goods throughout the world. Hunger and want would be banished, work would become more of a challenge rather than a require-- ment, and world peace would be assured. What was not taken into account was human greed.

Today, we see more hunger and want than ever before. The homeless, the jobless, the hungry and sick are not only more plen- tiful but are found in the midst of plenty, to such an extent that they pose a threat to the health and security of the entire world.

Against this background, one would expect that societies that placed people before property would have been insulated to some degree against the pitfalls of the predatory states that do not sufficiently check human greed. But this hasn't happened.

In Eastern Europe, people have become disenchanted with regimes which entrenched a political elite, a strangling bureaucracy, and an excessive military establishment.

I remember one time I was invited to speak at a May Day rally in Halifax. I got up and I said that I think that the working people throughout the world have a problem in that under capitalism they carry two monkeys on their back. One is the monkey of exploitation by the boss and the other is the monkey of bureaucracy. Under socialism, even communism, there's only one monkey on your back—the bureaucrats. That one monkey can sometimes grow as big as the other two monkeys, in which case the worker loses out both ways.

I'm greatly disturbed by reports coming out of socialist countries about privileges by members of the elite, the ruling class. The fight has to be continued, even under socialism, against bureaucracy. It's a constant fight.

We see the same thing in the labour movement; you have people making half a million dollars a year and you have unions that have gone from elected officers to appointments for life, like Ryan of the longshoremen's union. He got a few of his cronies to get up at a convention and say, "I move that Brother Ryan be president for life." Well, it became a joke among a lot of people, among our critics. They called him King Ryan. He's no longer an elected person. He's president for life. So we started to bring royalty into the family of labour.

In the Soviet Union today, you have a situation where the politicians and the bureaucrats have fallen into the trap of trying to compete with the United States, especially in terms of the military, to the point that it has slowed down the standard of living of the working class. The same thing has happened in the US although it hasn't manifested itself yet as badly. But a military economy won't work. You can't continue to go so far into debt because of military expenditures. Both superpowers have gone too far in terms of the money they've spent on the military and in space, to the point that it's now threatening the economy in both countries.

I'm surprised that the climax has come in the socialist countries first. I would have thought that the socialist countries could have afforded their military and space programs more than the

In 1981, when J.K. Bell received an award from the Canadian Industrial Relations Association, the Halifax Chronicle-Herald published the following editorial:

Bell: Labour's ringing voice

On any list of Maritime labour "greats," James K. Bell's name would figure prominently.

His is one of the clearest, most persistent, and most respected voices of the labour movement.

Thus it comes as no surprise that the Canadian Industrial Relations Association would have selected the veteran secretary-treasurer of the Nova Scotia Federation of Labour for its 1981 Honour Award, which recognizes outstanding contribution to the study or practice of industrial relations in Canada.

Jim Bell was a teenager when, in the tough days of the 1930s, he took his first step onto labour's stage—as one of the leaders of a group of immigrant quarry workers in Saint John. It was the baptism of fire that was to launch a career of union work in several of the provinces of Canada.

He was to become an executive member of a union of unemployed persons in Ontario. Later, he organized shipyard and marine workers in New Brunswick and Nova Scotia; served as secretary-treasurer of the Halifax–Dartmouth District Trades and Labour Council, and secretary-treasurer of the Marine Workers Federation. For years he has been a key figure in the Nova Scotia Federation.

He has fought for the unions in the courts, across the bargaining tables, and before labour boards. His has been an influential contribution to the briefs labour annually presents to government. And many of the reforms that have been written into our labour laws have been inspired by the advocacy of James Bell.

He has long been a leader for better housing, improved health and safety care at the workplace, equality of opportunity between male and female workers, greater pension protection for retired workers, modernization of workmen's compensation benefits, pension portability, and more labour input into decision-making levels of government and industry.

Perhaps more than any other man in Nova Scotia's labour movement, he is recognized as top man—"Mr. Labour."

US In reality, the socialist economies have not been able to provide both guns and butter to the same extent as the capitalist countries. The capitalist countries have been more able to go into debt, to mortgage our future than the socialist ones.

The corruptions of the past have left their mark on our youth, many of whom would sell their future for the plastic and tinsel values in the free market nations. It will be a difficult task to correct these values and this skepticism. Unless this happens, I fear the rise of neo-fascism and its right wing allies in Europe and the West which has already manifested itself in various ways.

Today, I'm searching for a socialist society. Every system has a peak and fruition. It has to be replaced by another system. You had slavery, you had feudalism, you have capitalism, but capitalism can't live forever. That's the way it is with social orders. No social order is the beginning and end of all social orders. Capitalism isn't that old. A lot of people are confused. They don't realize that capitalism is only of short duration. I don't believe any system will live for ever. Conditions will bring about its demise.

* * *

Since my retirement, I have occasionally been involved in union affairs, especially those involving the Marine Workers' Federation. I must acknowledge the help, over the years, of women who worked in the union office such as Mabel Adams, Pat Lavangie, Jenny Harding and Glenda Cooper, as well as others in adjoining offices.

I have also walked the picket lines with other union groups such as the craft building trades. When a number of them, along with the bakery workers led by René Quigley, got together to build a union building in Halifax, they decided to name the building in the Bayers Lake Industrial Park after me. That was a great honour.

During a trip to Halifax, I spoke to postal workers who had a sit-in underway in Dartmouth. I told them how the workers in the Fisher Body Shops of Flint, Michigan won their strike in the 1930s under the CIO. I also participated in the demonstration by PSAC [Public Service Alliance of Canada] in Halifax when they were on strike in the fall of 1991. I spoke to the crowd, and I said, there's nothing original about Mulroney. There's nothing original about his philosophy. Mulroney, in his concern for foreign workers as against his lack of concern for Canadian workers, has caved in to the continental programs of the US. He takes a militant attitude against the workers but not a militant attitude against those who would continue to exploit our natural resources and our labour movement.

He reminds me of an old trade unionist who got up at a CLC convention, and speaking of another person, he said, "Oh yes, that fella is militant enough. He's so militant that before he gets down on his knees to kiss the boss's arse, he demands that the boss take down his own trousers." That's about the militancy that Mulroney has in regards to other countries when it comes to safeguarding our jobs and our natural resources.

These problems are going to be compounded with global free trade deals whereby many Canadian enterprises will consider shifting production to cheap-labour countries. Trade unionism in Canada must restructure to meet this new threat and must develop unity and co-operation with other social groups such as co-ops, environmental groups, women's organizations, students, and native people. While unity may not be accomplished at all times, the basic common issues would be identified and advanced.

Those of us who spoke out against continentalism in the past and warned of the political give-away of our natural resources and subsequent loss of jobs, economic well-being, and political independence were branded as "troublemakers" and "radicals" by those who were actually giving the country away by the shipload.

Things are completely different today. I suppose I sound like an old fella spouting sour grapes, but trade unionists seem to be a different breed now. They're all business. They'll attend a union meeting and when the meeting's over, they pick up and go their separate ways. When we had a meeting, we were up until two in the morning at a Chinese restaurant. Things were much different then. There was more togetherness in the labour movement than there is today.

You talked labour. People wanted to know the latest news of what was happening in the labour movement across the country. You pumped one another as to what was going on, what problems were coming up, and about unions, personalities, what have you. You felt you were part of a movement. Today, you just belong to your own local and you don't care what the hell happens across the street.

When we went to a labour council meeting, for example, fellows would get up and explain the problems they were having with their employer. And we'd stay there until midnight listening to what they were saying, things they were putting up with in a particular industry. Today, there's more of a tendency in unions to not tell anyone, even another union, about what's happening. Keep it all as internal stuff. Half the time they don't even tell you that a unit or two of their organization is on strike in the very community.

Today, unions seem to be only concerned with their own problems. For example, there was this fellow who was always harping at federation conventions because we had to mimeograph material. At a convention, we would accept resolutions right up to the last minute so you couldn't always have them printed. You had to mimeograph them. I tried to explain that to him but he wouldn't listen. So finally I grabbed him by the lapels of his coat. I said, "Show me the union label on your coat." But he didn't have a union label anywhere. He didn't believe in any other union label except the printers.

People in the trade union movement used to be idealistic. They'd be out working, not on a paid basis but on a volunteer basis, to organize the unorganized. But no one gives a goddamn for the unorganized anymore. They're on their own.

Quite frankly, I'm a bit fearful for the future of the labour movement. I'm afraid that the workers and the unions and the unorganized workers are going to swallow the poison of the neo-fascists who are re-emerging on the scene today, and that we're in for a drift to the right.

Our trade union leaders in North America ape the boss. They want whatever the boss has—whether it's a plane or a car. In Europe or Great Britain, some of the labour leaders bicycle to work. They know where they come from and who they're leading. Our people here have the idea that the labour move-ment is a stepping stone to affluence. Some of the fellows here think you're not successful unless you have a Mercedes Benz and a hideaway apartment. Unfortunately, a number of their mem-bers think the same thing.

I think the trade union movement will have to go through a regeneration. We have to settle the whole question of foreign unions in Canada. We have to settle the overlap of jurisdiction of unions. We have an obsolete type of structure. And we have to adapt to global strategies that are being developed by govern-ments and by companies.

Am I optimistic? It all depends on how militant the workers become.

Selected Bibliography

Abella, Irving Martin. *Nationalism, Communism, and Canadian Labour: The CIO, the Communist party, and the Canadian Congress of Labour 1935-1956*. Toronto and Buffalo: University of Toronto Press , 1973.

_____ , *The Canadian Labour Movement, 1902-1960*. CHA Booklet No. 28, 1975.

Berger, Thomas. *Fragile Freedoms: Human Rights and Dissent in Canada*. Toronto: Clarke, Irwin & Co., 1981.

Berton, Pierre. *The Great Depression. 1929-1939*. Toronto: McClelland and Stewart Inc., 1990.

Buck, Tim. *Thirty Years. The Story of the Communist Movement in Canada 1922-52*. Toronto: Progress Books, 1952.

Calhoun, Sue. *A Word to Say: The Story of the Maritime Fishermen's Union*. Halifax: Nimbus Publishing, 1991.

Cameron, Silver Donald. *The Education of Everett Richardson: The Nova Scotia Fishermen's Strike 1970-71*. Toronto: McClelland and Stewart Limited, 1977.

Gilson, C.H.J. ed. *Strikes: Industrial Relations in Nova Scotia 1957-87*. Hantsport, N.S.: Lancelot Press, 1987.

Green, Jim. *Against the Tide: The story of the Canadian Seamen's Union*. Toronto: Progress Books, 1986.

Harrop, Gerry. *Clarie: Clarence Gillis, MP, 1940-1957. A Political Memoir: From the Coal Mines of Cape Breton to the Floor of the House of Commons*. Hantsport, N.S.: Lancelot Press, 1987.

Horowitz, Gad. *Canadian Labour in Politics*. Toronto: University of Toronto Press, 1968.

Kaufmann, Uwe K. *History of the Marine Workers' Federation*. Musquodoboit Harbour, N.S.: Karsten Press, 1987.

Livesay, Dorothy. *Right Hand Left Hand: A True Life of the Thirties*. Erin, Ontario: Press Porcepic Ltd., 1977.

MacEwan, Paul. *Miners and Steelworkers: Labour in Cape Breton*. Toronto: Samuel Stevens, Hakkert & Company, 1976.

MacEachern, George. *An Autobiography: The Story of a Cape Breton Radical*. David Frank and Donald MacGillivray (ed). Sydney, N.S.: University College of Cape Breton Press, 1987.

Seymour, Edward E. *An Illustrated History of Canadian Labour 1800-1974*. Ottawa: Mutual Press Ltd., 1976.

Smith, Stephen. "Cold War and Canadian Labour: A Case in Atlantic Canada." Paper for history 6300, David Frank, University of New Brunswick, April 24, 1984.

Stanley, Douglas C. *Industrial Inquiry Commission on Saint John Shipbuilding and Dry Dock Co. Ltd.* Fredericton, N.B., September 1972.

Trudeau, Pierre Elliott (ed.). *The Asbestos Strike*. Translated by James Boake. Toronto: James Lewis & Samuel, 1974.

White, Howard. *A Hard Man to Beat: The Story of Bill White, Labour Leader, Historian, Shipyard Worker, Raconteur*. Vancouver: Pulp Press, 1983.

White, Jay. "Pulling Teeth: Striking for the Check-Off in the Halifax Shipyards, 1944." *Acadiensis* XIX no. 1, Fall 1989.